OCR HISTORY A

The Development of the Nation State: France 1498–1610

Alastair Armstrong | Series editors: Martin Collier | Rosemary Rees

CW01024320

withdrawn 25/1/23

www.heinemann.co.uk

✓ Free online support
✓ Useful weblinks
✓ 24 hour online ordering

01865 888080

Official Publisher Partnership

Heinemann is an imprint of Pearson Education Limited, a company incorporated in England and Wales, having its registered office at Edinburgh Gate, Harlow, Essex, CM20 2JE. Registered company number: 872828

www.heinemann.co.uk

Heinemann is a registered trademark of Pearson Education Ltd

Text © Alastair Armstrong 2009

A no: 040974

C no: 944.02

First published 2009

12 11 10 09
10 9 8 7 6 5 4 3 2 1

British Library Cataloguing in Publication Data is available from the British Library on request.

ISBN 978-0-435-31264-0

Typeset by TechType
Original illustrations © Pearson Education Ltd, 2009
Illustrated by TechType
Cover design by Pearson Education Ltd
Cover illustration © AKG-Images/Museé Contonal des Beaux-Arts
Edited by Kirsty Taylor
Index compiled by Catherine Harkness
Printed in the UK by Henry Ling Ltd

Acknowledgements
The author and publisher would like to thank the following individuals and organisations for permission:

Photographs
© Art Archive/Bibliotheque des Arts Decoratifs: p. 30; © Mary Evans Picture Library: p. 45; © Corbis/Christophe Boisvieux: p. 52; © AKG-Images/Erich Lessing: p. 56; © Art Archive/ Chateau de Blois/Gianni Dagli Orti: p. 79; © Art Archive/Musee de Chateau de Versailles/ Gianni Dagli Orti (Henry, King of Navarre): p. 88; © Art Archive/Chateau de Blois/ Alfredo Dagli Orti (Marguerite of Valois): p. 88; © Alamy/The London Art Archive: p. 92; © Bridgeman Art Library/Bibliotheque Nationale Paris, France: p. 121.

Written sources
Pp. 60–61: The Rise and Fall of Renaissance France 1483-1610 © R. J. Knetch; p. 61: Louis XII of France: The Unlikely Lad by Glenn Richardson, History Review. Reprinted with permission of History Today Ltd.

CONTENTS

HOW TO USE THIS BOOK

This book is a study of the developments in Renaissance and Reformation France and focuses on the extent to which France became a nation state during this period.

Features

There are many features in the margins of the book which are directly linked to the text and will help stimulate the students' imagination and pick out key information.

Key Terms – these pick out and define key words.
Key People – these give a brief biography of important people.
Key Themes – these pick out important themes, either of the time or of historians studying this period.
Key Concepts – these highlight important concepts.
Key Events – these give a brief overview of important events.
Key Places – these give brief explanations of why certain areas are important for this topic.
Exam Tips – these give important hints and tips for exam success.

Exam Café

The text in the book is supplemented by an exciting **Exam Café** feature. The Exam Café is split into three areas: Relax, Refresh, Result!

- **Relax** is a place for students to share revision tips.
- **Refresh** your memory is an area for revising content.
- **Result** provides examiner's tips and sample answers with comments.

Planning and Delivery Resource

The Development of the Nation State: France 1498–1610 chapter of this resource contains guidance and advice for ways to approach and teach this topic for the OCR specification. There are student worksheets which help to build up source skills for the examination requirements. This also contains lots of additional source material and an Exam Café with more tips, sample answers and detailed examiner commentary.

INTRODUCTION: SIXTEENTH CENTURY FRANCE

Reims Cathedral The place where French kings were traditionally crowned. The coronation ceremony itself was an elaborate and symbolic affair in which the archbishop of Reims anointed the king with holy oil handed down from heaven by a dove at the baptism of King Clovis (king of the Franks in 481) and used ever since in the coronation ceremony. The anointing symbolised the power and almost God-like status of the French king.

KEY TERMS

Renaissance monarchy
Renaissance monarchs are those in the fifteenth and sixteenth centuries who embraced the rebirth of classical literature and artistic styles that occurred throughout Europe. In France, the period 1498–1559 is viewed as the high point of Renaissance monarchy: great French kings such as Francis I promoted the strength and status of monarchy through architecture, literature and the splendour of court. A chivalric and at the same time enlightened outlook was required and therefore war in Italy against the Habsburgs coincided with great palace building on the Loire Valley and patronage of important scholars.

WHAT WAS THE FRENCH KINGDOM LIKE IN 1500?

On 27 May 1498 Louis, Duke of Orleans, was crowned King of France in **Reims Cathedral**. The circumstances of his succession were fortuitous in that his predecessor and cousin, Charles VIII, had stumbled and hit his head on a doorway entrance while on his way to watch a tennis match in the royal château at Amboise. With no immediate male heirs, the crown passed to Louis, thus beginning what many historians have termed a period of **Renaissance monarchy**, in which Louis reformed the legal system, reduced taxes and expanded French territories in Italy. In 1498, when Louis took his coronation oath, in which he promised to defend both Church and kingdom, France was some way from being a unified nation-state.

Indeed Frenchmen barely recognised their country as one whole unit, simply because there were few common traits of national identity to bind the kingdom together. French frontiers were vague; no common language existed; and the country's system of law was not unified. European nationalism and the concept of a nation-state developed only fully in the nineteenth century, although we can trace the development of modern France throughout the early modern period. However, it would be foolish to believe that successive French Renaissance monarchs set out to unite the country: there was no grand plan to push France towards a nation-state. Instead, monarchs such as Louis XII and Francis I recognised the link between a more centralised government and increased royal authority.

The process of overcoming parochial, provincial barriers was a slow and not entirely successful one during the sixteenth and seventeenth centuries:

- Of all early modern European kingdoms, France had the greatest area (459,000 square kilometres), the largest population (approximately 15 million) and the richest agriculture, yet government was decentralised and relatively weak.

- The economy was largely rural: over 80 per cent of the population were based in the countryside, although urban populations were on the rise by the sixteenth century. Economic depression in the second half of the sixteenth century, made worse by the French Wars of Religion, hit the rural population hard.

- The three major towns of Paris, Lyons and Rouen had populations over 60,000 and were among the largest towns in western Europe. The cities served as centres of trade, administration and intellect where new ideas could spread through word of mouth or by the newly developed printing press. Nevertheless, local customs and traditions along with poor internal communications prevented French trade from reaching the levels of its maritime neighbours in this period.

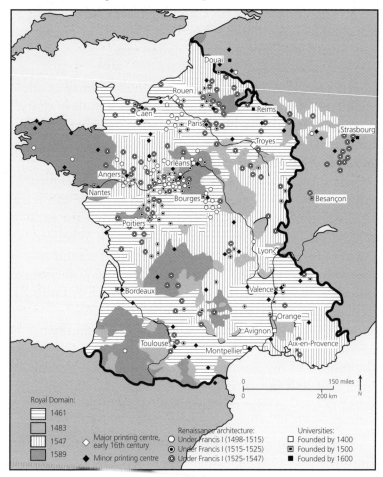

Renaissance France

Moreover, the makeup of the French kingdom had been altered relatively recently by the assimilation of frontier provinces such as Burgundy in 1491. Indeed, in 1500 nearly one-quarter of the kingdom had been acquired in the previous 50 years. Therefore, much of France was new, acquired by diplomacy, conquest or marriage. Metz, Toul and Verdun in 1522 and Calais in 1558 are further examples of territories that became part of the French kingdom in the sixteenth century. Much of the credit for this unification of France goes to the French king, Francis I.

Yet, to describe France as a nation-state would be false for the following reasons:

- Few Frenchmen regarded their country as a unified whole: **provincial liberties** often overrode central directives.
- The Hundred Years' War had ended only in 1453, and during that conflict much of the realm had been occupied at one time or another by English or Burgundian troops. Only when the English were defeated and removed from the south-west of France did French rule resume for the first time in 300 years.
- Burgundy, Picardy and Provence were all acquisitions made by the French crown since 1470. Clearly the assimilation of such important territories increased the power of the crown and began to form the boundaries of modern France. Renaissance monarchs in France continued this process throughout the sixteenth century, and made efforts to impose the royal will on such provinces. Yet, declaring royal authority and passing legislation in such territories was one thing, actually translating that will into practice was another.
- In reality such newly acquired provinces could not easily become part of the French kingdom. They had their own histories, traditions and privileges that were now under threat from the crown.
- New **parlements** were established in Dijon, Bordeaux, Rennes and Rouen throughout the sixteenth century in order to ensure that the royal prerogative was carried out. These were provincial replicas of the Paris *parlement*,

but they met with mixed success, especially during periods of weak monarchy.

Still, the medieval adage of 'one king, one faith and one law' largely rang true in France. In many ways these were the principles that bound French society together. Despite separate customs and traditions, all Frenchmen in 1500 looked to one rightful king appointed by God, followed the one true faith of Catholicism and abided by the law of the land. Yet it seems impossible to talk of 'Frenchmen': few regarded themselves as such; rather they were Bretons, Normans or such like. While a French monarch existed, many provinces ignored royal legislation if they could and avoided paying taxation to the crown if at all possible. The arrival of Protestantism in the sixteenth century shook French society to the core, challenged the old values and beliefs of Catholicism and fuelled over 30 years of civil war. Royal authority rose under the Renaissance monarchs, fell during the Wars of Religion and recovered again in the seventeenth century, reaching a pinnacle under Louis XIV. Therefore, throughout the period, all three tenets of 'one king, one faith and one law' were challenged and out of turmoil and tragedy emerged the beginnings of the modern state that we recognise as France.

WHO WERE THE FRENCH KINGS IN THE SIXTEENTH CENTURY?

Louis XII (King of France, 1498–1515)

Louis XII was known as the 'Father of the People' as a consequence of his relatively lenient taxation demands. Louis married Anne of Brittany (widow of Charles VIII), having attained an annulment of his own previous marriage to the daughter of Louis XI. Later he would marry Mary Tudor, sister of Henry VIII. His military adventures in Italy were fruitless and he was eventually driven out of Lombardy by the Holy League of England, Spain, the Pope and Holy Roman Empire. His reign is seen by many as the cross-over from mediaeval government to Renaissance rule. It certainly extended the authority of the crown but still relied upon traditional power bases in the localities. Louis contributed to the formation of a nation

EXAM TIPS

The nature of the examination paper that you are studying for is synoptic and thematic. This means that you need a broad, general overview of the key events and individuals that shaped the sixteenth century in France. One of the key themes will be the development of the French monarchy over the course of the period 1498–1610. It is therefore useful to have some idea from the beginning of the course just who these kings were and how effectively they governed.

state primarily through his marriage to Anne but also through the creation of a more efficient administrative government.

Francis I (King of France, 1515–47)

Francis was a notable patron of the Renaissance, presiding over a court which attracted some of the finest artists, architects and thinkers in Europe. He was the nephew and son in law of Louis XII, from whom he inherited the Italian Wars against the Habsburgs. Success in war was perceived as a reflection of monarchical power and Francis I's reign got off to a good start when he seized Milan in 1515 after the Battle of Marignano. Subsequently Francis put himself forward for the title and position of Holy Roman Emperor in 1519 after the death of Maximilian but lost out to Charles (V). In 1525 Francis was taken prisoner by Charles after suffering a humiliating loss at the Battle of Pavia. He was only released in 1526 having renounced Flanders, Artois, Burgundy and Italy. Ultimately Francis lost out to Charles at the Treaty of Cambrai (1529) and Crepy (1544) showing that the logistics of holding on to Italy were beyond France. Francis I's foreign adventures also meant a steady increase in domestic taxation. At home the Concordat of Bologna (1516) confirmed royal gallicanism (royal control over Church appointments) whilst the Affair of the Placards (1534) marked a more defined policy towards heresy. Francis enhanced royal authority, and eroded provincialism. He generally had the upper hand over representative institutions and in this respect one ought to view Francis as authoritarian rather than consultative.

Henry II (King of France, 1547–59)

Henry was the son of Francis I and at the age of 14 he married the Italian princess, Catherine de Medici. They would, in time, produce seven surviving children of which three would become kings of France (Francis II, Charles IX and Henry III). Henry II carried on the theme of reform and centralisation in government with mixed success. He further contributed to the shaping of modern France through the aquisition of Metz, Toul and Verdun for the French kingdom in the ongoing duel with Charles, but saw his army annihilated by that of the young Philip II at St Quentin in 1557. The return of Calais from England in 1558 removed another foreign enclave from France, although the Peace of Cateau Cambresis one year later gave up all French claims to northern Italy. Henry II had to deal with the onset of Calvinism and like his predecessors he showed little mercy to heretics. Henry established the Chambre Ardente to prosecute and punish those of the new learning, although Calvinist numbers continued to grow even in the face of such harsh measures. His premature death in a jousting accident in 1559 left Catherine and his three young sons to deal with noble faction and the growth of Protestantism, thus showing the fragility of monarchical power in France in the sixteenth century.

Francis II (King of France, 1559–60)

Francis was a boy king (age 15) on his succession and was married to Mary Stuart (later Queen of Scots). His short and sickly reign was dominated by his wife's uncles, the Duke of Guise and the Cardinal of Lorraine. Francis was the subject of an audacious kidnap attempt by French Calvinists at Amboise in 1560 which failed. At a time when France needed strong authoritarian rule, they only had a boy. Francis died of an ear abscess in 1560, thus shifting the balance of power once more at court.

Charles IX (King of France, 1560–74)

Another boy king (age 10) on the throne entailed a regency government headed by Charles IX's mother Catherine de Medici who governed until he came of age in 1563. Guise influence was lessened but Catherine's policies of toleration for Calvinists soon led to serious problems and ultimately civil war. Charles increasingly came under the spell of Admiral Coligny (a Calvinist noble) at court and the King has traditionally been viewed as weak and indecisive. Such traits were partly to blame for the St Bartholomew's Day Massacre of 1572 in which thousands of Huguenots were murdered on the streets of Paris.

Henry III (King of France, 1574–89)

Henry III inherited a France riven with faction and civil war. Henry was unable to inflict defeat on the Huguenots and as a consequence he lost the faith of Catholic nobles. His rule was increasingly undermined by the Guise family, especially after the death of Henry III's brother, Anjou in 1584. The Catholic fear of a Protestant succession radicalised the cause and gave new impetus to the Catholic League led by the Duke of Guise and funded by Spain. The Catholic cause was divided between Leaguers and Royalists. Henry was barricaded out of Paris in 1588 by Guise, underlining the depths to which monarchical power had sunk. Henry tried to restore authority by desperate measures, having Guise murdered in December 1588. Henry himself was assassinated in the following summer. He died childless, thus the Valois line ended with him and a succession crisis ensued.

Henry IV (King of France, 1589–1610)

With the Valois line extinct, the succession passed over to the Bourbons. The problem for most Frenchmen was that Henry of Navarre was a Calvinist and had been the key military figure in the Protestant cause since the 1560s. Henry set about convincing France that he could rule as king by defeating the Catholic League, appeasing key nobles, declaring war on Spain and most importantly renouncing Calvinism in 1593. Henry was the architect of the conciliatory Edict of Nantes (1598) which formed the legal basis of the settlement with the Huguenots. Henry and his key minister Sully put France back on the road to financial stability and rebuilt the authority of the crown. In this respect Henry IV was shrewd and skilful although he was also aided by the general war weariness of the populace.

THE DEVELOPMENT OF FRANCE AS A NATION STATE

Over the course of the period 1498–1610 France begins to develop into a nation state. That is to say that a decentralized collection of provinces begins to emerge as a unified nation, and the people of France begin to perceive a national identity of sorts. The transition from a late medieval state based around the monarchy to a more modern dynastic state starts to take place in the sixteenth century, although we do have to take into account the chaos of the second half of this period in which civil war severely sets back the process. Over thirty-five years of religious war goes some way to explaining why the transformation into a nation state took so long in France. Before we go any further in this discussion it is crucial to understand just what we mean by the term 'nation' in the sixteenth century, as its meaning differs considerably from the modern definition. A nation state in the early modern period, required fixed territorial boundaries and was built upon a shared culture and common social organisation. A codified legal system and linguistic unity also helped to foster a sense of nationhood. That none of these characteristics were in place in France in 1500 goes to show how much needed to be done before one can talk of France as a nation, and by 1610 there was still some way to go. Given the nature of government in the sixteenth century, the monarchy was likely to be a key institution in the forging of a nation state. Certainly the desire of strong monarchs such as Francis I and Henry IV to extend their authority over the whole kingdom helped (albeit unwittingly at times) to bring together a very loosely connected group of territories into a more centralised and recognisable state. Yet the triumph of absolute monarchy in the seventeenth century and the establishment of a nation state was not a straightforward process, and the trials of the monarchy in the sixteenth century demonstrate the significance of religious unity amongst other factors to the development of nationhood in the early modern period.

OVERVIEW TABLE OF SPECIFICATION KEY THEMES

Specification key theme	Analysis	Key evidence and turning points	Page reference
Nation state	• France lacked the key hallmarks of a nation state in the sixteenth century such as defined territorial boundaries, linguistic and legal unity and a sense of nationhood.	• Codification of the legal system under Barme and Baillet	29
	• Over the course of the first half of the sixteenth century, the acquisition of territories such as Brittany by the crown served to create the modern hexagon shape of France, yet few people thought of themselves as French. Local dialects and different languages continued to exist despite the gradual advance of French in legal and academic circles.	• Concordat of Bologna, 1516	36
		• Acquisition of Brittany, 1532	28 and 31
	• The codification of law began under Louis XII but customary laws still existed in the south of France and local traditions and privileges continued to be upheld.	• The Edict of Villers Cotterets, 1539	48
	• The Wars of Religion exacerbated particularism and undermined monarchical attempts at centralisation. Religious developments served to undermine national unity and divide the nation at political and social levels. Foreign intervention in the Wars of Religion also served to undermine the idea of a nation state.	• The Edict of January, 1562	77
		• St Bartholomew's Day Massacre, 1572	91
		• The Catholic League receive Spanish aid, 1584	108
	• Between 1562–98 religious concerns and loyalties took precedence over any sense of national identity.	• Henry IV declares war on Spain, 1595	121
	• By the end of the period, France was still some way from becoming a nation state. The whole concept of national identity was something which did not truly emerge until the eighteenth century, yet one could argue that the peace and stability brought about by Henry IV laid the foundations for further progress towards the development of a nation state.	• The Edict of Nantes, 1598	130

OVERVIEW TABLE OF SPECIFICATION KEY THEMES

Specification key theme	Analysis	Key evidence and turning points	Page reference
Relations between king and subjects	• The power of the French monarchy fluctuated over the course of the sixteenth century. Renaissance monarchs, namely Louis XII, Francis I and Henry II exerted strong, personal kingship. • The reigns of these strong monarchs were characterised by increasingly centralised government, religious unity and a symbiotic relationship with the nobility. • French kings rarely ruled in the interests of their subjects. The third estate had no political representation and was taxed heavily throughout this period. The monarchy relied upon the nobility to maintain order in the localities. • Relations between the king and the nobility changed somewhat over the course of this period due to the increasing sale of royal offices (venality). This created a new bureaucratic class of nobles called the nobility of the robe, which arguably challenged the old nobility. In reality the old nobility remained important and retained their status. Many of the offices sold were merely cosmetic and brought with them little political power. • Relations between the king and the nobility changed more drastically as a consequence of religious divisions. Disproportionate numbers of nobles supported Calvinism and undermined the sacred nature of French kingship. In the 1580s Leaguer Catholics also shunned the monarchy as a consequence of its failure to extinguish heresy. The French Wars of Religion significantly weakened the authority of the French monarchy. • Monarchical power was restored somewhat under Henry IV at the end of the period, and his reign laid the foundations for a strong French crown in the seventeenth century.	• Louis XII re-organises the Grand Conseil, 1497 • Concordat of Bologna, 1516 • Bourbon Rebellion, 1523 • Closure of the Rouen Parlement, 1540 • Death of Henry II, 1559 • Outbreak of the French Wars of Religion, 1562 • Huguenot Resistance Theories, 1573–79 • Death of Anjou, 1584 • The Day of the Barricades, 1588 • Henry of Navarre abjures, 1593 • Edict of Nantes, 1598	29–30 36 45–46 47 72–73 78–79 96 107 111 120 130–31

OVERVIEW TABLE OF SPECIFICATION KEY THEMES

Specification key theme	Analysis	Key evidence and turning points	Page reference
Religious developments	• In the first half of the sixteenth century France was united under Catholicism both at a social and political level. Socially Frenchmen were united as a community of believers. Politically, the French king ruled as God's representative on earth.	• The symbolism and significance of the coronation ceremony	13–15
	• This unity was shattered by the emergence of Calvinism in the 1540s and the 1550s. Despite harsh persecution, Calvinism continued to grow in strength and attracted key noble support.	• The nature of the French Church	15–16
		• The Affair of the Placards, 1534	41–42
	• The outbreak of religious war in 1562, split France on religious lines and heralded over thirty-five years of ruinous civil war.	• Noble Support for Calvinism	66
	• At a social level communities were divided and instances of popular religious violence occurred. At a political level the nobility were divided and the authority of the crown eroded.	• The Edict of January, 1562	77
	• The failure of the crown to extinguish heresy was a key factor in the weakening of its authority. By the 1580s, a rival institution known as the Catholic League emerged under Spanish and Guise control. Its main aim after 1584 was to maintain the Catholicity of the French Crown.	• The St Bartholomew's Day Massacre, 1572	94
		• Spanish aid for the Catholic League, 1584	108
	• Henry IV's reign brought about a period of peace and stability although religious problems were only partially addressed.	• The Edict of Nantes, 1598	130–31

OVERVIEW TABLE OF SPECIFICATION KEY THEMES

Specification key theme	Analysis	Key evidence and turning points	Page reference
Social and economic developments	• In the first half of the sixteenth century, France was relatively prosperous based on economic recovery after the end of the Hundred Years War (1453) and demographic growth after the ravages of the Black Death in the fourteenth century.	• The position of the French nobility	17–18
		• The position of the Third Estate	23–24
	• France suffered something of a mid-century crisis. Economic growth gave way to stagnation and recession. The causes of this downturn can be found in the heavy borrowing of the French monarchy, an influx of silver from the Americas, harvest failures and above all else ruinous civil war.	• Louis XII reduces the level of the taille	30
		• Western Rebellion, 1542	44
	• The results of this depression were unemployment, landless peasants, inflation and poverty stricken lesser nobles.	• The Bourbon Rebellion, 1523	45–46
	• The Wars of Religion ensured that France felt the effects of depression more severely than other European states.	• The power of the nobility	60–61
	• Henry IV's reign marked something of a recovery, based on domestic peace and a readiness to invest in the communications infrastructure.	• Opposition to the salt tax in Bordeaux, 1548	57
	• The third estate suffered most during this period. Although relatively well off during the first half of the sixteenth century, population growth and heavy taxation made peasants' lives very hard indeed. At times of acute hardship the peasantry were forced to raise arms against the oppression of their local lords.	• Peasant Revolts, 1579	104–05
		• Peasant Revolts, 1593–95	124
	• Historians identify the second half of the sixteenth century as a period of crisis for the old nobility. Challenged by the emergence of the nobility of the robe, divided amongst themselves by religion and hit hard by the economic depression it can be argued that the power of the French nobility declined. That said, this outlook is too general and whilst some lesser nobles did have to sell off land it was the older nobility of the sword who possessed the wealth and land to withstand the depression.	• Biron (1601) and Bouillon (1606) Rebellions-	139–40
		• Sully's restoration of the economy	133–34

CHAPTER 1

How was France governed in the period 1498–1610?

INTRODUCTION

One of the central themes in any study of sixteenth- and seventeenth-century France is the rise of monarchical authority: a steady growth in power under strong Renaissance monarchs was followed by a rapid decline during the Wars of Religion (1562–98), before it recovered once more under the steady hand of Henry IV to reach its zenith of absolutism in the seventeenth century under Louis XIV. In hindsight, the process looks straightforward and simple: in reality there was no grand plan for absolutism and the development of France into the most powerful state in Europe in the seventeenth century was more complex than it seems. Monarchical attempts to extend royal power and centralise government predictably met with some opposition, and the development of a nation-state highlighted the limitations of royal authority as well as the strengths.

HOW POWERFUL WAS THE KING OF FRANCE?

Nevertheless, at the heart of the kingdom in 1500 was the king, and it was through him that policies and developments relating to language, culture, religion and war were driven. During periods of weak monarchy, such as the minority rule of Charles IX, control over such means of development was limited. Imagery and ritual were all-important in developing the concept that French kings were appointed and ordained by God to rule over the kingdom, and selling this idea to their subjects was a major part of royal propaganda.

French kings were not only ordained by God but were themselves thought of as gods. Myths developed around their sacred powers; for example, one touch from the French king after his coronation would allegedly cure the horrible skin disease scrofula. Such ritual was an important part of the relationship between king and subject, as it reinforced the idea that royal authority was sacred. Moreover, each new French king was anointed with the holy oil of the sacred ampulla which linked that king to all his predecessors. Thus the ancient and sacred nature of French kingship was visible in the ceremony. After consecration the king was presented with his crown, sceptre and regal vestments. The king's duties were outlined in his coronation oath, namely to promote peace, protect his subjects, dispense justice fairly and expel heretics from his kingdom. The king also received the eucharist in both kinds, that is both the bread and the wine, a measure only received by the clergy. Again, the purpose here was to boost the king's secular and sacerdotal status. The royal propaganda of the sixteenth century portrayed the king as a divine ruler and the one man capable of unifying the diverse elements that made up the French kingdom.

Yet sixteenth-century France was largely feudal and the king, for all his power and prestige, still had to respect the rights of his subjects. Provinces, towns, guilds, nobles, the church and corporations all enjoyed a measure of independence. Often Frenchmen owed greater allegiance to province than to realm, as the former was so remote from the centre of power. Particularism, then, was a major problem for French kings in the early modern period, and, despite patronage and careful management, attaining the unstinting loyalty and submission of their subjects was often impossible. Throughout the period 1498–1610 notions of royal absolutism evolved which envisaged a French monarchy free of external restraints such as councils or *parlements*, and with all power vested in one man. According to this doctrine, the king was appointed by God as his viceregent on earth: it was the king's right to make laws, dispense justice and create offices. Any institution which curbed or eroded royal authority could be abolished under the royal prerogative and local traditions and privileges could only remain with the king's consent.

Lawyers and humanists throughout the sixteenth century, such as Guillaume Bude and Jean Bodin, articulated this theory and successive French kings sought to fulfil the role of absolute monarch. There were opponents to this theory, such as Claude de Seyssel who put forward three restraints on royal power, namely religion, justice and established ordinances. Seyssel was still advocating royal authority, but in a different context. In practice, however, the king of France remained bound by certain obligations and rights with regard to his subjects and administrative machinery was necessary to oversee the effective rule of the kingdom.

WHAT WAS THE IMPORTANCE OF THE CHURCH IN FRANCE IN THE SIXTEENTH CENTURY?

The symbolism of the coronation ceremony emphasised the unique relationship between the French monarchy and the Catholic Church. The French king had the papal endorsement of *rex christianissimus*, the 'Most Christian King'. Moreover, the French Church operated virtually independent of Rome after the passing of the Pragmatic Sanction of Bourges in 1438 which increased Gallican liberties and curbed papal intervention. The sanction allowed cathedral chapters to elect both bishops and abbots independent of royal and papal control. Gradually, however, this clerical Gallicanism was impinged upon by the crown, a process accelerated by Louis XI who was essentially controlling clerical appointments himself by 1471. Such practice was officialised in 1516 by the Concordat of Bologna which gave Francis I the right to nominate candidates directly for vacant bishoprics and archbishoprics thus increasing the power of the crown over the church, and giving rise to what one may describe as royal Gallicanism. With such power of appointment and as recognised guardian of the Church it was to the king rather than the Pope that Frenchmen looked to for spiritual protection. Yet royal Gallicanism also allowed for corruption in terms of clerical appointments and, as in other parts of western Europe, the church witnessed lowering standards of education and practice. Few of the bishops appointed by either Francis I (1515–47) or Henry II (1547–59) had any theological training, with only three out of 80 appointments made by the latter monarch having a degree in theology. On the other hand, control of clerical appointments gave French kings great power and allowed them to distribute their patronage among the nobility and reward Italian allies of the French who opposed the Habsburgs.

Calls for reform of the Church emanated from learned humanists such as Jacques Lefèvre d'Étaples who rejected scholasticism and instead focused on improving the Christian life through education, a return to the original scriptures and moral reform. Lefèvre soon joined with a like-minded humanist named Guillaume Briconnet, bishop of Meaux, and the humanist Circle of Meaux was born. The scriptures were read to parishioners in the mother tongue while Lefèvre d'Étaples translated the New Testament into French in 1523. Although all participants in the circle were orthodox Catholics and loyal to their king, the group came under suspicion in the 1520s because of the actions of **Luther in Germany**: despite the patronage of Francis I's sister Marguerite, it was suppressed in 1525. Whether we regard the Circle of Meaux as a forerunner to reform or not, the issue of reform and heresy became a more pressing one for successive French kings after Francis I. As reformist views became more radical, persecution was stepped up and, although the German Luther made little impact in France, French native **John Calvin** had much greater success operating from his base in Geneva.

French Protestantism emerged as a strong minority in the 1550s and divided the kingdom and weakened the monarchy until the conclusion of the French Wars of Religion in 1598. Ultimately, to the vast majority of Frenchmen, Catholicism was the one true faith, and heresy was intolerable. The failure of French monarchs in the second half of the sixteenth century to defeat the Huguenots on the battlefield and stamp out Protestantism led to a decline in the fortunes of the crown both at a political and popular level.

Catholicism tied the king to his subjects and bound the nation together as a community of believers. The Church legitimised the king's authority, and tied him to his subjects. The eucharist and the mass lay at the centre of people's lives as much in a social sense as doctrinally. Therefore, Protestantism represented a serious political and social threat as well as a spiritual one.

KEY EVENTS

Luther in Germany Under the spiritual leadership of an Augustinian monk from Saxony, Martin Luther, a popular movement emerged that challenged the doctrine and teachings of Catholicism. This became known as the Lutheran Reformation and is viewed as the first concerted and serious challenge to the Catholic Church in Europe. It was only really successful in northern Europe but its impact was felt all over the continent.

KEY PEOPLE

John Calvin (1509–64)
Born in Noyon, Picardy in north-east France, Calvin was the founder of a more influential branch of Protestantism than Luther. Forced to flee from France in 1535, he lived in Geneva. He worked tirelessly to spread his religious message across Europe and his work *Institution de la Religion Chrétienne* (Institutes of the Christian Religion) was the first clear and structured presentation on the doctrine of Protestantism.

WHAT WAS THE ROLE OF THE NOBILITY IN SIXTEENTH-CENTURY FRANCE?

The nobility held a privileged and powerful position within French society. As French nobles did service to their king on the battlefield they were exempt from direct taxation. Therefore, those who could afford to pay most, actually paid least. They had seigneurial rights over the peasantry which meant that they acted as landlords towards the peasantry and as independent judges. The leading nobility in France were known as the *noblesse d'épée* (or the **nobility of the sword**) because of their military obligations to the crown, and membership of this exclusive club relied upon the ability to trace family lineage back for at least two centuries. Indeed, the crown became increasingly eager to pass legislation prohibiting people from just claiming noble status without actually holding a title. The rather fluid nature of social mobility at the beginning of the sixteenth century meant that many rural landlords had merely assumed noble status, and begun living nobly, exempting themselves from taxation and therefore depriving the crown of income. At the head of the nobility of the sword were the royal princes of the blood and beneath them dukes, peers, cardinals and marshals all with varying degrees of wealth and prestige. In 1469, Louis XI created the order of St Michael the Archangel, a chivalric order that grouped together the most important nobles in the realm. A hierarchy was beginning to develop within the nobility itself, shaped by the crown. The result was that the leading noble families were showered with distinctions and royal patronage, consequently increasing their power and status. The lesser nobility found it increasingly difficult to survive, and during periods of hardship many slipped back into the third estate (see below). Indeed, the aristocracy as a whole was coming under threat and no little criticism at the beginning of the sixteenth century for a number of reasons. Enlightened humanist opinion portrayed them as barbaric, interested only in military adventures and their own worldly ambitions rather than learning and the fate of others.

In the early sixteenth century, the house of Bourbon was the most powerful of all families. Founded in the fourteenth century, the family held large amounts of land in central France and as with other such nobles the territories were very much the demesne of Charles of Bourbon, who effectively ruled over the provinces. In 1515, Charles was made constable of France which made him leader of the French army in peacetime. While this might be viewed as an effective use of the king's patronage, a crisis arose in 1521 on the death of Bourbon's wife, the Duchess Suzanne, who had actually inherited all of the Bourbon lands herself in 1488, and married her cousin Charles in order to unite the two branches of the family. Suzanne's will naturally left all of the Bourbon land to her husband but its validity was challenged by Louise of Savoy, the King's mother, on the grounds that she was Suzanne's nearest blood relative. The claims were put before *parlement*s, but in the meantime the King began to dispose of Bourbon lands, selling them for profit. In 1523, Charles turned against his king and allied with France's most bitter enemies, namely Charles V of Spain and Henry VIII of England. While Francis was in Italy, Charles led a rebellion with English and Imperial aid. The plot was uncovered and Charles forced to flee the kingdom in disgrace. Bourbon lands were assigned to the crown, a transfer which became almost permanent on the death of Charles at the sack of Rome in 1527. Power factions were, therefore, a constant source of trouble for French monarchs in the early modern period. Moreover, such factions were exacerbated by the fact that a relatively large number of nobles, including the Bourbons and Châtillons, were attracted to Calvinism in the second half of the sixteenth century. Such support, often based on political or financial profit, gave Calvinism the necessary legitimacy and power it required to survive amid persecution and served to lengthen the Wars of Religion.

The final major development within noble ranks during this period is the emergence of the *noblesse de robe* (or **nobility of the robe**) in the sixteenth century. The concept of venality, the sale of offices for royal profit, created thousands of new administrative and bureaucratic positions which were eagerly snapped up by ambitious gentry or merchants keen to better themselves. Although the new nobility could not challenge the social prestige of the old nobility, they were an increasingly attractive prospect to French kings. The downside to venality was that it created further layers of bureaucracy which hampered royal authority.

Of course, the royal court became an increasingly important source of power and patronage for the French nobility. Royal titles, jobs, money, land, tax-farming contracts and contacts became the prizes on offer for those wealthy and important enough to reside at court and receive the king's patronage. From a monarchical perspective, it has been argued that court became an important control mechanism for the king, somewhere that nobles were compelled to reside and where they could be closely monitored. During the Wars of Religion the relationship between the king and the nobility broke down entirely as the balance of power swung back towards the localities. Indeed, the frequency of noble revolts against the crown throughout the sixteenth century testifies to the fact that the nobility represented a powerful body of opinion and at times an obstacle to the extension of monarchical power.

HOW WAS FRANCE GOVERENED IN THE SIXTEENTH CENTURY?

During the sixteenth century, there were three main organs of government in France, namely the king's council, the grand *conseil* and the *parlement* of Paris. The king's council, once made up entirely of the princes of the blood, the peers of the realm and other great magnates, was, by the sixteenth century changing in its composition as French monarchs sought to guard against noble domination. Trained lawyers and clerics increasingly found royal favour and the king also personally selected an inner council (*conseil d'affaires*). Here in the inner cabinet crucial policy decisions on matters such as foreign affairs were made.

Since 1497, the grand *conseil* had also grown in stature with regard to judicial activity, and fixed membership allowed for continuity and stability. The grand *conseil* acted as the king's own portable law court, following him on his travels and adjudicating on appeal cases or complaints against royal officials. The chancery made the council's decisions into law through royal enactments, but as royal legislation increased, greater responsibility was handed to officials under the control of the chancellor and attached to the royal council, namely the *maîtres des requêtes*. Trained in the law, these officials served to link departments of administration and the majority were ennobled for their service.

Of the seven *parlements* which existed, the oldest, most powerful and most prestigious was the *parlement* of Paris. It acted as the highest law court and its jurisdiction covered two-thirds of France; although still considered part of the king's council, the *parlement* regarded itself as the guarantor of liberty and acted as a check on royal authority. All royal legislation had to be ratified by the *parlement*, and remonstrances or objections to the king were not uncommon. If *parlement* continued to object, the king might himself attend the court in person and preside over the ratification of the law in question, a measure known as a *lit de justice*. Such actions were rare and were often viewed as the trait of a weak monarch. The six provincial *parlement*s were largely a result of France extending its boundaries in the fifteenth century, and the provinces of Toulouse, Bordeaux, Dijon, Grenoble, Aix and Rouen all had institutions based on the Paris model. Each *parlement* held sway in its own province with regard to ratification of legislation.

The only elected national body was the **Estates General** which was made up of representatives of the clergy, nobility and third estate. With the right to ratify treaties and approve taxation, theoretical power was great. Yet the Estates General tended to meet only in times of crisis and on the king's authority. It was never summoned under Francis I or Henry II, and it met on only five occasions between 1560 and 1615. Therefore, the Estates General was largely inconsequential in reforming French government and its inactivity highlighted the failure of the French nobility to fulfil a crucial political function as a consequence of religious division and faction.

The Estates General A national representative body made up of elected representatives from the clergy, nobility and third estate. Called by the king, usually to discuss and debate matters of critical importance.

Local or provincial government was based around the provincial estates which, unlike the Estates General, played an influential role in the distribution of finance and the regulation of taxes and customs duties. Provincial governors, drawn from the ranks of the aristocracy, were important figures of authority in the eleven border provinces of France. The powers of the provincial governor were vague, however, and often the post was used as a reward for good service to the crown; furthermore, often the governor spent more time at court than in the province. Ultimately, the king could hire and fire governors at will and French monarchs were wary of appropriating too much power and authority to influential and ambitious individuals far from the centre of royal authority. Beneath provincial governors came the **baillis**, who were in control of the 86 *bailliages*. At a local level, the *bailliage* was an important facet of government and one which was open to corruption from officials who were poorly paid.

> **KEY TERMS**
>
> **Bailli** A local royal official whose job it was to ensure that the royal decree was carried out in that area (*bailliage*).

A major trend in government administration in the sixteenth century was the creation of offices and an increase in the level of bureaucracy. Francis I had one office holder to every 3,000 inhabitants, a reflection not only of the increase in royal business in institutions such as the chancery (the body which turned council decisions into law), but also of the lucrative nature of venality.

HOW EFFICIENT WAS THE TAXATION SYSTEM IN SIXTEENTH-CENTURY FRANCE?

Ordinary revenue from sources such as the king's crown lands together with extraordinary revenue from taxation made up the king's annual fiscal haul. Annual revenue fluctuated and difficulties in the collection of taxation reflected the decentralised nature of the kingdom. The **taille** was the direct tax, levied annually and in two forms. The *taille personnelle* was based upon the individual's ability to pay while the *taille réelle* was a land tax and applied to all social ranks and was unquestionably fairer. Yet the *réelle* was used only in certain areas such as Languedoc and Provence. From the reign of Charles VII, French kings could tax at will, although it must be remembered that the nobility and clergy were exempt from the *taille* as were other groups such as lawyers and royal officials. In fact, the burden of taxation fell upon the peasantry and the sixteenth century saw a number of sporadic but

> **KEY TERMS**
>
> **The taille** The main direct tax in France levied on those who could afford to pay least, namely the third estate (or peasantry).

nevertheless significant peasant uprisings against taxation. Indirect taxation also existed; one example being the *gabelle*, a tax on salt, a crucial commodity for the preservation of food. The aides were similar duties on commodities sold regularly and in large quantity, such as wine or livestock.

Given the decentralised nature of the French kingdom, collection of taxation became a thorny issue for the French crown. Exemptions, both noble and provincial, reduced the number of people who could be taxed, while effective collection in outlying provinces proved difficult. Arrears often accumulated in times of war when levels of taxation were higher. Various measures were introduced throughout the sixteenth century in an attempt to increase the efficiency of tax collection in the provinces. Royal agents represented the culmination of such efforts and while ministers such as Sully did much to enhance the amount of money returned to the royal coffers, the same problems continued to exist, exacerbated in the sixteenth century by civil war.

Effective tax assessment and collection was further hampered by provincial traditions and privilege. While in the *pays d'élections* tax was levied by royal administrators on orders from the royal council, in the *pays d'états* taxation was levied by the local estates. Therefore, in provinces such as Brittany, Languedoc and Provence the responsibility for levying taxation fell on local estates rather than the crown, a privilege that was fiercely defended by these territories, and a clear obstacle to uniformity, efficiency and national identity. While the *taille* was assessed and collected by an elected representative, the right to collect indirect tax was auctioned to the highest bidder. The victorious bidder was allowed to collect and keep the tax in question after prior payment of a fixed sum to the crown. Therefore, the opportunity for profit and corruption were vast, although it did ensure a regular return from the provinces for the king with few administrative problems. In general, the *taille* brought in about 2.4 million **livres** out of a total revenue of 4.9 million; the aides contributed 0.8 million livres; the *gabelle* cashed in 6 per cent of the total revenue.

HOW DID ORDINARY PEOPLE LIVE IN SIXTEENTH-CENTURY FRANCE?

The **third estate** is a general term to describe all those who did not belong to the noble or clerical classes. At the upper end of the scale were wealthy merchants, royal office holders and lawyers: men of ambition who perhaps had designs on ennoblement. In an urban context there were also artisans and lesser merchants who could count on a comfortable income and standard of living. Yet the vast majority of the third estate were peasants. France was an overwhelmingly rural society with only one person in twenty living in a city of over 10,000 inhabitants. The vast majority of French men and women lived in small village communities dispersed throughout the kingdom. Communal spirit was created by the intimacy of village life, the parish church, public farmland and general co-operation among villagers. That is not to say that movement from villages was static during the course of the sixteenth century. Indeed, new opportunities to buy land elsewhere or earn higher wages in another village encouraged movement. Consequently, cheap land and favourable tenancy rates saw the rise of a wealthy middle class within the villages throughout the first half of the century. Thereafter, rising taxation, split inheritance, the dislocation caused by civil war and poor harvests changed the dynamic of the village again. In this environment, a very small number of very wealthy farmers prospered on the back of financial reserves and connections. The gap between rich and poor widened between the village elite and the day labourers.

In the lead up to the sixteenth century, the lot of the peasant had improved considerably. Between 1450 and 1560, after the ravages of the Black Death and the Hundred Years' War in the fourteenth century, the French population had almost doubled. Consequently, there was an upsurge in agriculture to meet the growing demand for grain. Land clearance and reclamation provided territory for cultivation while the emancipation of serfs gave incentives for labour. Yet by the mid-sixteenth century grain production failed to keep up with the demographic increase and scarcity soon led to inflation and starvation.

Moreover, wages failed to keep up with rising grain prices and there was a surplus of workers on the land. Small peasant holdings were often sold to pay back debts, a trend which was exacerbated in the second half of the sixteenth century by the Wars of Religion. Often such land was bought by the landlords and it was a case of the gap between rich and poor increasing. Unemployment, vagrancy and begging were commonplace in sixteenth-century France and towns witnessed an increase in populations as the poor sought work. With the constant burden of taxation upon their shoulders, life for the peasant was hard, and over 35 years of civil war made it no easier.

Peasant unrest was frequent as a consequence of economic hardships brought about by landlords looking to make as much profit as possible out of their relatively short land leases, poor harvests, and taxation. Local hardships brought about by economic depression often led to sporadic outbursts of popular protest. Often the revolt was aimed at hated royal tax collectors or agents of the crown in the provinces, as they were perceived to be encroaching upon the parochial liberties of rural life. The larger peasant revolts often culminated in an attack on the local town, and increasingly peasant revolts appeared to become better organised and focused. At times, force and aggression were used to quell the rebellion and dissuade others from carrying out similar actions. The extent to which French monarchs actually cared about the well-being of their subjects as monarchical power increased is debatable. Despite the various hardships and traumas of the sixteenth century, and the increasing fiscal pressures imposed by the crown, the peasantry appeared to get on with life, subdued through fear and a sense of knowing their lot within the social hierarchy, into general political ignorance and apathy. Only when their immediate interests came under threat or life became intolerably hard did they make their voice heard, and then their actions could be an unwelcome distraction for the crown and royal troops might be deployed.

CHAPTER SUMMARY

The specification key themes across the period can be summarised as follows:

Nation state

France did not exist as a nation state in 1500. Each province fiercely guarded its own traditions and privileges. Particularism was slowly eroded throughout the period by acts such as the codification of law and the increased use of royal agents in the localities, yet this was insufficient to create a sense of nationhood.

Relations between kings and subjects

Royal authority fluctuated between the Renaissance strength of Francis I and Henry II to the weakness of Charles IX and Henry III during the civil wars. A period of recovery and centralisation along similar lines to the beginning of the sixteenth century marked the reign of Henry IV. The use of venality to boost the royal coffers and fund war increased, thus widening the number of people involved in royal bureaucracy. A new noble class, the nobility of the robe, arguably emerged to challenge the traditional political power of the ancient nobility. Yet the old nobility of the sword, remained crucial to the monarchy and their social status remained intact.

Religious developments

France was united under Catholicism in the first half of the sixteenth century, but the rise of Protestantism in the 1550s threatened the Gallican principles on which the authority of the crown and the order of the nation depended. Above all other factors religion served to divide France in the sixteenth century.

Social and economic developments

Warfare, both foreign and civil during this period, placed an often intolerable tax burden on the third estate who were already facing pressures of inflation and land shortage by the mid-sixteenth century. With the nobility exempt from taxation, it was the third estate who suffered most, and at times of acute distress peasant unrest and violence was not uncommon. The division between rich and poor continued to grow during the sixteenth century. Fluctuations in the economy over the course of the sixteenth century were as a consequence of many factors such as the cost and effects of war, the weather and royal intervention. Economic change and its impact are crucial in the development of France as the effect on society was often marked. Increased taxation might lead to popular unrest whilst inflation could result in a drop in standards of living. One would expect a nation state to have a uniform economic outlook with some form of centralised agricultural and industrial identity. However despite some progress to centralise the state around the monarchy in the first half of the century, industry and agriculture stagnated and declined, partly as a consequence of civil war (1562–98).

QUESTIONS TO CONSIDER

1. In your own words define the term *sacred kingship*.

2. Why might any challenge to the authority of the Catholic Church upset domestic order and peace in France?

3. What was the role of the nobility in sixteenth century France?

4. How powerful were representative institutions such as the *parlements* and the Estates General?

5. What was life like for ordinary Frenchmen in the sixteenth century?

CHAPTER 2

Renaissance monarchy 1: Does Louis XII deserve the title 'Father of the People'?

LOUIS XII, KING OF FRANCE, 1498–1515

What was Louis XII's background?

Louis was born in 1462 during the reign of his second cousin Louis XI. His father was Charles, Duke of Orleans, head of a branch of the royal house of Valois. Louis XI was succeeded by his son Charles VIII in 1483. Louis of Orleans became heir and got on well with the new King.

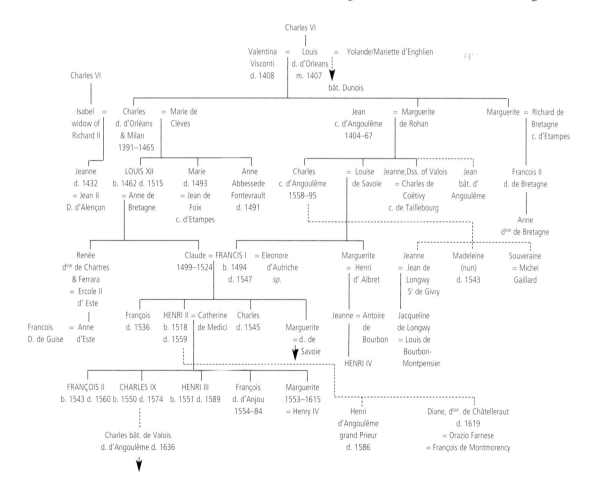

Orleans – Angouléme family tree.

Yet, the King's sister Anne of Beaujeau was determined to dominate the King's favour alongside her husband, the Duke of Bourbon. Therefore, in 1485 and again in 1488, Louis was forced to join forces with other discontented nobles, most notably the Duke of Brittany, and rebel against the crown. Captured in 1488, Louis was never charged with treason and by 1491 amicable relations with Charles had been restored. So, Louis' background was one of controversy and disorder, and there were even rumours surrounding his legitimacy to rule. However, in May 1498 Louis was crowned king in Reims Cathedral and with little political experience began a rule which lasted nearly seventeen years and did much to set France on the road to legal codification and political centralisation.

HOW DID LOUIS XII CONSOLIDATE HIS POWER?

Louis' first priority was to secure his position as king and ensure that no opposition to his rule emerged. To this end he ended his first marriage to **Jeanne**, daughter of Louis XI, and married **Anne of Brittany**, widow of Charles VIII and eldest daughter of Duke Francis II of Brittany. The marriage served an important political function:

- It consolidated the French absorption of Brittany (although it was not until 1532 that the duchy was formally attached to the French kingdom).
- It allied Louis to a powerful noble family.

Like his contemporary in England, King Henry VII, Louis was wary of noble faction and he was careful not to exclude important nobles from court while also ensuring that they were not able to build up independent power bases. Therefore, Pierre de Rohan, *Seigneur de Gie* and prominent member of the Bourbon family, became an important royal adviser. Accused of treason in 1504, Rohan fell from power, probably the victim of trumped up charges orchestrated by Cardinal George d'Amboise and the Queen, both of whom were jealous of Rohan's influence with the King.

KEY TERMS

Ordinance of Blois, 1499
This was a royal edict that attempted to lessen corruption within the judicial system and bring fairer and more uniform justice to all. Magistrates practising in the law had to be properly qualified and judicial offices had to be earned rather than purchased. Many of its terms were repeated in the Ordinance of Lyons in 1510, which suggests that it made only limited impact on the ground.

Louis also made attempts to extend his power and authority into the provinces, thus centralising government and controlling his nobility. In 1499, he issued the **Ordinance of Blois**. This was followed in 1510 by the Ordinance of Lyons. Such edicts may be taken as evidence of Louis XII's willingness to reform and in particular to define clearly the powers of regional officials and make them accountable to the crown. There were other changes that seemingly heralded political and social change:

- Louis set about codifying French law. This was crucially important in the creation of a French nation state as it meant that unwritten, provincial customary laws were slowly replaced with a more official, coherent and uniform set of customs. Louis XII commissioned two *parlementaires*, Roger Barme and Thibaut Baillet to write down the customs of northern France. By the end of Louis XII's reign their job was almost complete but the rest of France would have to wait longer for their customs to be officialised.

- A new *parlement* was established in Provence and in Normandy the main law court or *Echiquier* was made into a permanent body. Under Francis I it would become the Parlement of Rouen. Louis had made small inroads into the parochial nature of French government.

- Louis' reign also witnessed the beginnings of change in the social hierarchy and marked the emergence of a new noble class, the so-called nobility of the robe (see page 18). Legal reforms created new offices which in turn brought ennoblement for those who were appointed to judicial positions. However, we should not exaggerate the extent of change. In reality the ancient nobility of the sword (see page 17) was still the major source of power and prestige within France, and the idea that Louis created legal offices in order to undermine the great magnates is false.

- In 1497 Louis reorganised the Grand Conseil or king's council. The Grand Conseil acted as an itinerant royal law court. Louis XII gave it a permanent staff of legal experts capable of defending the royal prerogative in territorial disputes. Such an initiative strained royal relations with the *parlements* who felt undermined by the new status of the Grand Conseil. To **placate the** **parlementaires** Louis allowed them to sit in the Grand Conseil whenever they wished.

Noble families such as La Trémoille were an important part of Louis XII's regime and in many ways their support was crucial in maintaining law and order in the localities. Louis worked closely with the nobility, and several assemblies of notables reflect the close relationship which existed between the king and this estate. Little aristocratic opposition during the reign of Louis XII bears testament to a relatively consultative and conciliatory approach towards the nobility.

How effectively did Louis XII manage his finances?

Louis had been left a deficit of 1.4 million livres by his predecessor and cousin, Charles VIII. In turn, Louis handed on the same deficit to his successor, Francis I. Therefore, while Louis was unable to actually make a profit, he did manage royal finances relatively effectively:

- He was also able to reduce the level of the *taille* (see page 21). In 1500 the *taille* amounted to only 2.3 million livres, as compared to 3.9 million under Louis XI. Such a move was most popular and went some way to earning him the title of 'Father of the People'.
- In order to compensate for such a reduction he increased the levels of indirect taxation, and exploited church and noble wealth. In 1504 and 1508, Louis introduced financial reforms designed to improve the collection of taxation and the accountancy process.
- Although technically illegal, Louis XII continued the royal trend of selling offices to nobles and wealthy merchants. This was known as venality and served as a useful and quick cash expedient for the crown.
- He made some inroads into levels of corruption in the practice of tax collection through the appointment of eight royal officials, the *gens de finances*, whose job it was to oversee the collection of revenue. Such officers of the crown also increased royal influence in the localities.

Louis had made a start in the process of effective fiscal management, but given the diversity, size and decentralised

Placate the **parlementaires** A key theme throughout the sixteenth century is the relationship between the monarch and representative institutions. Here we see an early example of the king working with the *parlements* but relations would not always be so amicable in the future as kings sought to exert their authority.

Louis XII, 'Father of the People'.

nature of the kingdom, progress was always likely to be slow and limited. Eight officials would not make a huge difference, and local tax farmers were still making vast profits at the expense of the masses.

How far was George d'Amboise able to reform the Church?

Louis XII endorsed a programme of Church reform under Cardinal George d'Amboise, a royal minister and papal legate. Amboise focused on the regular clergy, carrying out visitations of monasteries and other religious houses.

- Great abbeys such as Fontevrault were given thorough inspections and necessary reforms relating to moral conduct and spiritual practice were carried out. Smaller monasteries were put under the control of larger ones for guidance and direction to try to prevent disrepair in the future.
- The extent of reform was limited. The King relied upon enthusiastic and energetic reformers such as Amboise but individual prelates could only achieve so much and clerical opposition to reform was fierce.

Who would succeed Louis XII?

- Queen Anne only produced a daughter, namely Claude. The King's closest male relative and nearest heir to the throne was his second cousin Francis d'Angouleme, who was only six years old in 1500.
- The King was faced with two marriage prospects for Claude. One was to see Claude married to Francis and thus maintain the Breton alliance with the crown whilst the other was to see her marry Charles of Ghent, infant son of Archduke Philip and grandson of Emperor Maximilian.
- Anne was firmly behind the Charles of Ghent marriage as it would preserve the independence of Brittany. The only possible advantage to Louis was the dowry which would bring with it Milan. Otherwise Brittany, Burgundy and Blois would all be lost with the marriage, leaving France territorially divided.
- Whilst in public the betrothal of Charles of Ghent to Claude was celebrated, in private Louis was having second thoughts. In May 1506 the Charles of Ghent match was repudiated and Claude was betrothed to

Francis. By 1512 it was clear that Anne was not going to produce a son, and Francis was admitted to the king's council in anticipation of his future kingship.

In preventing the Charles of Ghent match Louis had preserved the make up of the French kingdom and prevented the loss of Brittany. He also used the **Assembly of Notables** skilfully to justify his decision. In May 1506 at Plessis-lez-Tours the delegates of the Assembly implored the King to marry Claude to Francis for the good of the kingdom. Of course Louis had set the whole meeting up but he used this as a justification for repudiating the Treaty of Blois with Maximilian which had promised Claude to Charles of Ghent.

KEY TERMS

Assembly of Notables A group of clergy, nobles and royal office holders personally selected and summoned by the king to consult on national affairs

CHAPTER SUMMARY: HOW FAR HAD FRANCE PROGRESSED TOWARDS BEING A NATION STATE DURING THE REIGN OF LOUIS XII?

What trends can we see developing?
- Louis XII attempted to make royal government more effective and centralised, although the reality of the situation on the ground was markedly different to official policy. Some historians argue that a modern monarchy was emerging under Louis XII, whilst others suggest that he continued to rely upon the medieval mechanisms of government.
- Louis XII continues the Italian Wars of Charles VIII and commits France to costly campaigns.
- Partly as a result of these costly campaigns, Louis expands methods of raising revenue beyond the *taille*.

The specification key themes across the period can be summarised as follows:

Nation state
Louis married Charles VIII's widow, Anne of Brittany in 1499, which facilitated the incorporation of Brittany into the French kingdom. Such territorial acquisitions were a crucial part of defining the modern shape of France and should be viewed as an important development in the move towards a nation state. Furthermore, customary laws

EXAM TIPS

It is crucial to understand the condition, identity and make up of France in 1498 if one is to understand how things changed (or not) thereafter. You need to identify trends that begin under Louis XII and then you will be able to see the extent to which these patterns/themes continue over the next chapters.

were codified under Barme and Baillet, bringing some form of judicial uniformity to the kingdom.

Relations between kings and subjects

Louis XII extended the authority of the crown over the provinces and in doing so went some way to centralising the power of the crown. In lowering the *taille*, Louis XII attained the title, 'father of the people' suggesting that he cared about the welfare of his subjects. New *parlements* were established in the localities and the Grand Conseil was professionalised. These were developments that suggested a more modern, bureaucratic style of kingship, yet Louis continued to rely upon the nobility of the sword to maintain law and order in the localities. Louis XII's use of an Assembly of Notables in 1506 to confirm the marriage of Claude (his daughter) to Francis demonstrates the importance of the nobility in legitimising and supporting key decisions.

Religious developments

With little in the way of heterodox opinion emerging during Louis XII's reign, France remained united under the banner of Catholicism. That is not to say that the Catholic Church was necessarily in good health, and an unfulfilled programme of Church reform under George d'Amboise hints at some of the failings within the late medieval French church.

Social and economic developments

Louis XII ushered in a period of relative stability and prosperity. The rate of the *taille* was lowered, easing the burden on the third estate, although levels of indirect taxation and venality increased. Generally Louis XII's reign witnessed a period of economic recovery after the devastation of the Hundred Years War (1337–1453). Population levels were increasing after the ravages of the Black Death in the fourteenth century, but there was still plenty of land to go around, and it would appear that the third estate were relatively content and prosperous during this period.

QUESTIONS TO CONSIDER

1. In what ways did Louis XII attempt to centralise French government?

2. Did Louis XII's reign begin Renaissance monarchy in France or was the kingdom still governed along feudal lines?

3. What obstacles existed to effective government in France during the reign of Louis XII?

CHAPTER 3

Renaissance monarchy 2: Francis I

FRANCIS I, KING OF FRANCE, 1515–47

KEY THEMES

Historical Interpretations
Interpretations of Francis I's
reign have attempted to gauge
the extent to which he
centralised the French
kingdom and whether or not
he paved the way for
seventeenth century
absolutism. In *A History of
France 1460–1560*, David
Potter sees the rule of Francis
in the context of those that
preceded him and believes
that he continued the gradual
erosion of particularism which
Louis XI and others before
him had begun. In *The Rise
and Fall of Renaissance France*,
R. J. Knecht sees Francis as a
catalyst towards constitutional
unity and centralisation, while
still recognising the
limitations of his rule, most
notably with regards to
foreign policy which
contributed to the decline of
France in the second half of
the sixteenth century.

What was Francis I's background?

Francis was fortunate to become king in 1515, in the sense that Louis XII could reasonably have been expected to have fathered a son from one of his three marriages. On his accession to the throne, Francis was 21 years old, and in many ways he fitted the image of a Renaissance monarch perfectly. Tall, strong and athletic, Francis had a passion for war, literature, architecture and art. During his reign, countless châteaux such as that at Chambord in the Loire Valley were constructed, while Francis also built up one of the finest libraries in western Europe. He was no scholar but he was well read in ancient mythology and he was a great conversationalist.

Francis was born on 12 September 1494 in Cognac. His father was Charles, Count of Angoulême, and his mother, Louise, was the daughter of Philip, count of Bresse. Much like his English counterpart, Henry VIII, Francis preferred hunting or jousting to bureaucracy. Still, major decisions especially those concerning foreign affairs were overseen by the King and substantial parts of each morning were spent being briefed on current affairs and proposing policy to be discussed in the ***conseil des affaires***, although such routine was regularly disrupted by war.

KEY TERMS

Conseil des affaires The
inner cabinet of the king's
council made up of his most
trusted advisers. It was here
that major policy decisions
were taken.

RELIGION AND HUMANISM

How far did Francis I increase the power of the monarchy over the Church in France?

When Francis became the king of France in 1515, the relationship between Church and state was in theory governed by the Pragmatic Sanction of Bourges of 1438. This was an agreement between the king and the Pope allowing cathedral chapters to elect bishops and abbots independently. The relationship between Rome and the

French Church was called Gallicanism and French clerical liberties were proudly guarded. Yet, the supposed guardian of these liberties, the king, had effectively taken control of the clergy by the beginning of the sixteenth century.

How far did the Concordat of Bologna (1516) increase the power of the Crown?

The **Concordat** of Bologna resulted from the political context of the beginning of the sixteenth century. Francis needed papal support in order to consolidate victory over the Swiss at Marignano on 14 September 1515, while Leo X was eager to restore some semblance of papal authority in France. The Pragmatic Sanction of Bourges was torn apart in 1516, to the horror of the *parlement* of Paris and the Gallican church. By the new agreement the king was legally able to nominate candidates directly for vacant bishoprics and to fill vacancies in abbeys and monasteries. In return, Leo could collect taxation from newly appointed bishops and he had the right to veto any of Francis' nominations. Two issues seem to be important here:

- The Concordat of Bologna gave Francis unprecedented control over the French Church. That said, it ought to be recognised that monarchical control over appointments had been steadily growing over the previous century. In this light the concordat merely officialised the process.

- *Parlement* was virtually forced to agree to the concordat despite bitterly opposing the extension of royal authority. Through threats and intimidation, Francis exerted his will upon the *parlement* of Paris.

The impact of the concordat

One of the unfortunate effects of the Concordat was the way in which Francis used his powers of appointment as a means of patronage, rewarding leading nobles with clerical positions. Of the 129 men appointed by Francis nearly 100 were related to leading aristocratic families. Few had any theological training and the extension in royal authority over the Church contributed to the declining standards of the French Church. Moreover, Henry II continued the practice of his father in appointing Italians to leading positions in the Church as a source of political patronage

Pluralism is holding a number of posts at once.

Simony is the buying and selling of Church privileges.

Nepotism is getting jobs for one's family.

Desiderius Erasmus (1466–1536) The most prominent and famous of the Christian humanists. Born in Rotterdam, Erasmus spent six years in an Augustinian monastery before becoming private secretary to the bishop of Cambrai and a priest (1492). He moved to England, where he became professor of divinity and Greek at Cambridge. In 1509, he wrote a satirical attack on the wealth and corruption of the Church entitled *In Praise of Folly* and in 1516 he produced a translation of the Greek New Testament. Reform from within and the revival of learning were the principles by which Erasmus worked. He and others like him laid the intellectual foundations for the Reformation by heightening awareness of scripture. Nevertheless, Lutheran doctrine such as justification by faith alone was too radical for Erasmus and his split from Luther was marked by the work *On the Freedom of the Will*, 1525.

in order to advance the French position in Italy. Absenteeism, **pluralism**, **simony** and **nepotism** were rife and it is hardly surprising that calls for reform were heard in the early sixteenth century.

What was the importance of French Christian humanism?

In the early sixteenth century, a movement emerged which answered contemporary calls for reform of the Church. This movement existed at a high academic level and became known as Christian humanism.

- Humanists sought to improve Christian life and worship through a return to the original scriptures and a better understanding of God's wishes.
- Men such as **Desiderius Erasmus** believed that the simple gospel message, the word of God, had been obscured by scholarly interpretation and indeed clerical ignorance.
- The humanist agenda was a spiritual renewal based around retranslation of the scriptures and moral reform of clerical practice.
- Some historians have described the humanist movement as pre-reform in that much of what these men put forward was carried one stage further by more radical Protestant reformers. The difference is that the humanists wanted reform from within the Catholic Church and had no wish for a split.

Jacques Lefèvre d'Étaples

The foremost Christian humanist in France at the beginning of the sixteenth century was Jacques Lefèvre d'Étaples from Picardy:

- Lefèvre returned to the original scriptures, editing and writing commentaries on the Latin **Vulgate Bible**, starting with the Psalms in 1509 before publishing an edition of St Paul's Epistles in 1512.
- Some scholastic theologians attacked Lefèvre for questioning the authority of the Vulgate, but his response was that he was merely revealing the true meaning of the scriptures as God had meant.

- Lefèvre became increasingly significant in France, especially after 1516 when he joined with Guillaume Briçonnet in the latter's bishopric at Meaux.
- An intellectual circle developed around Lefèvre and Briçonnet which included like-minded clerics and scholars. An emphasis was placed upon the scriptures and preaching, while devotional superstition was rejected.
- Travelling preachers endorsed the evangelical message across the diocese, led by Briçonnet and his vicar-general Lefèvre. In 1523, Lefèvre published a French translation of the Gospels and the entire New Testament.

In reality, the intellectual Circle of Meaux was no threat to the church; men such as Lefèvre were trying to reinvigorate Catholicism.

How radical was the Circle of Meaux?

On the whole, Lutheranism made little impact in France but from 1518 Luther's books were being smuggled into the country and were read eagerly by scholars, humanists and clerics. In 1521, the **Sorbonne** believed Lutheran influence strong enough to have his books outlawed and his doctrines condemned. From this point on, the Circle of Meaux came under suspicion as even the most moderate of reformers risked being labelled heretics, or Lutherans:

- First charged with heresy in 1523, Briçonnet responded with a traditional explanation of Catholic doctrine and instructed his preachers to be conservative in their sermons.
- At court, the King's sister, Marguerite of Angoulême, had one of the circle, Michel d'Arande, preach in her territories in Alençon and Bourges.
- Certainly some members of the circle were more radical than others and most were critical of popular devotional practices such as the cult of saints or indulgences.
- Royal protection preserved the circle until 1525 when the King was held captive after the French defeat at Pavia. The Sorbonne and *parlement*s of Paris dissolved the group, and Lefèvre was forced to flee to Strasbourg.
- Briçonnet stood trial, but was saved by the return of Francis I in 1526. Francis promptly put an end to

Vulgate Bible The Latin translation of the Christian Bible, originating with Jerome who attempted to provide an alternative to the confusing array of Old Latin versions. Vulgate means the common edition and it became the official Latin text of the Catholic Church. Reformers and humanists doubted the authority of the Vulgate and questioned its translation. They also placed an emphasis on vernacular (mother-tongue) scriptures.

The Sorbonne The Sorbonne was a college of the University of Paris, in particular the theological faculty. The traditional and conservative Sorbonne allied with the *parlement* and saw humanists such as Lefèvre and Briçonnet as heretics, in the same way as Luther was. In some ways, they were justified in their concerns over Meaux as men such as Guillaume Farel were more radical and the young Louis de Berquin had been caught with Lutheran literature in 1523. Yet Berquin had not been burned because Francis regarded him as a Renaissance man of letters.

proceedings and allowed his sister to recall the exiles, Lefèvre being made tutor to the royal children.

The problem in religious policy was that Francis and the Sorbonne differed in their outlook on what constituted heresy. Francis's toleration of humanism marks him out as enlightened. Francis was no Protestant sympathiser, and not even a convinced evangelical (see page 42), but he was not going to allow the Sorbonne to dictate religious policy and he was determined to protect the humanist circle.

To what extent was Francis in control of religious policy?

The powers given to Francis by the Concordat of Bologna meant that the king's decision mattered most and, as long as the humanists did not openly attack Catholicism or hold views that were clearly heretical, he was unlikely to act against them. Yet, as religious dissenters became more common and radical throughout France, the conservatives became more vigilant and active.

(see page 42)

KEY TERMS

Iconoclasts More extreme Protestants believed that the Catholic Church was ruled by the Devil and that religious decorations contravened the commandment against idolatry. The destruction of such images is called iconoclasm and the people who carried out the destruction are called iconoclasts.

KEY PEOPLE

Guillaume Farel (1489–1565) An original member of the Circle of Meaux. In 1528, he rejected Lefèvre and Luther in favour of Zwingli and headed to Switzerland. Working from Neuchâtel, Farel made it his goal to convert his homeland to the reforms of Zwingli.

In 1528, Duprat, Archbishop of Sens, proposed a harsh series of penalties for convicted heretics. In the same year, a statue of the Virgin Mary was deliberately damaged by radical **iconoclasts** in Paris. The number of Protestants in France was low, but sporadic events such as this kept the authorities on their guard. Francis himself paid for a new statue in silver and heeded warnings that such events signalled a radicalisation and popularisation of the reform movement. Many humanists such as **Guillaume Farel** turned to Zwingli, the Zurich reformer who denied entirely the real presence of Christ in the eucharist and saw the mass as purely commemorative.

However, as Protestant sympathisers became more extreme Francis still sought to protect the intellectual, moderate reform movement which he had patronised throughout the 1520s. Tensions between *parlement*, Sorbonne and Francis continued to grow, as the two former institutions attempted to clean up the court of those suspected of heresy. Attention turned once again to Berquin, who was tried in 1528 before a jury which ought to have been sympathetic towards him, as it was appointed by the Pope under orders from Francis.

Yet with the King out of Paris the Sorbonne bullied Clement VII into removing the commissioners and a new, more conservative group was appointed. With the Italian Wars going badly, Francis was in no position to act and Berquin was found guilty of heresy. When Berquin appealed to the *parlement* he was once again found guilty and burned on the Place de Grève.

Another member of the original Circle of Meaux, namely Gerard Roussel, was targeted in 1533, and accused by the Sorbonne of preaching heresy. Indeed, Roussel had preached a number of sermons in Paris during Lent which had attracted over 5,000 listeners, and some of the content had caused alarm among conservatives. Once more, royal protection was at hand for Roussel as Francis set up his own commission of enquiry and silenced those who wanted to see Roussel stand trial. Altogether, there was little to suggest that Francis had altered his rather ambiguous policy on heresy in 1533, and the protection of men such as Roussel encouraged more radical strains to develop.

One instigator of reform, Nicholas Cop, was moved to act on All Saints' Day 1533. Cop was the new rector of the University of Paris, and he used his traditional address to criticise the persecution of evangelicals and endorse the simple preaching of the gospel. **Cop's sermon** caused a great stir among the Sorbonne who likened Cop's doctrine not only to that of Lefèvre but also to that of Luther. Cop, fearing for his life, was forced to flee to Switzerland. The sermon set off a wave of persecution in Paris sponsored by the Sorbonne; there were more than 50 arrests. On his return to the capital, Francis took a more measured approach, ordering the Bishop of Paris to stop the persecution. It was clear that it was Francis who controlled religious policy.

KEY EVENTS

Cop's sermon Some historians have suggested that the co-author of the Cop speech may have been the future beacon of the second wave of reform, John Calvin.

KEY TERMS

Evangelicals Those who believe in the authority of scripture. In the sixteenth century, they advocated reform based on the word of God. Generally, evangelicals were more moderate than Protestants.

KEY EVENTS

Affair of the Placards
Paris was not the only city to experience the placards: several other regional capitals witnessed them as did the King himself, who reputedly awoke to find a placard on the door of the royal bedchamber in Amboise.

Edict of Coucy, 1535
Francis was eager to consolidate his alliance with the Schmalkaldic League and the fierce repression of heresy did not look good to men such as Philip of Hesse. An alliance was not forthcoming in 1535 yet despite this Francis opened up the pardon to Zwinglian sacramentarians in 1536.

To what exent did the Affair of the Placards mark a turning point in Francis I's religious policy?

Once more the **evangelicals** were confident that if they progressed at a slow pace and maintained royal support they could survive and prosper. Yet the situation changed on the night of 17–18 October 1534 (the **affair of the Placards**) when placards (posters) were put up all over Paris attacking the mass and in particular the Catholic doctrine of transubstantiation:

- The placards were crude and violently offensive, attacking the Catholic Mass.
- They attacked priests as the antichrist and transubstantiation as the doctrine of devils.

Such abuse played straight into the hands of the conservatives who used the affair to push the King towards taking a harsher line on heresy. Cop's sermon had been evangelical and humanist in nature; the placards were blatantly heretical. The author of the placards was Antoine Marcourt, a Frenchman living in Neuchâtel, Switzerland. The immediate consequence of the placards was a severe period of repression driven by the Sorbonne and this time backed by Francis I. Marcourt and his supporters represented a small minority in their views but the consequences of their actions severely dented the ambitions of a larger minority of evangelicals. The period of repression saw 24 executions and the passing of numerous edicts encouraging citizens to inform upon heretics in the community. Informers would receive one-quarter of their victim's property and possessions. Massive religious processions were staged in Paris to demonstrate the orthodoxy and commitment of the Most Christian King, while all book printing was banned. The persecution did not end until 16 July 1535 when the king proposed the **Edict of Coucy** which released religious prisoners and offered amnesty to exiles (except supporters of the placards) if they promised to admit their errors within six months.

There are three main points to make about the Affair of the Placards and its consequences:

- The placards did not necessarily harden Francis's line on heresy as he had never tolerated such a doctrine, but they did move him to act against radicals, and in some ways clarified the division between reform and heresy.
- Protestant and evangelical reformers were in a very small minority in France in the 1520s and early 1530s, operating in secret and underground. Cop's sermon and the placards were exceptions to this, but because they were such high-profile cases the consequences were far-reaching. **Protestantism became seen as the religion of rebels** and a threat to the national order which had to be eradicated.
- By 1536, Francis had offered a pardon to all heretics provided they abjured within six months, thus demonstrating that his position had not been greatly altered by the placards. He still wished to pursue a middle line if possible, although he had become more aware of radical elements within the reform movement which threatened to undermine his rule.

Protestantism as the religion of rebels At the beginning of this period in France religion served to underpin the authority of the crown. The growth of Protestantism undermined the power of the monarchy.

To what extent did heresy become a greater threat to Francis I in the period 1538–47?

The Truce of Nice (1538) freed Francis from the need to court the German princes, and Francis recognised that greater powers over heresy needed to be given to the *parlement* in order to isolate French Protestants at home and prevent them from contacting those in exile:

List of condemned books The list drawn up by the Sorbonne contained 65 titles with works from Luther and Melanchthon featured, as well as those by John Calvin.

- The Edict of Fontainebleau in June 1540 gave the *parlement* overall control of heresy jurisdiction, reflecting just how much headway Protestantism was beginning to make in France.
- In 1543, ecclesiastical authorities were given more powers to search and arrest subjects.
- Also in 1543, Francis ordered the Sorbonne to draw up a Catholic Confession of Faith, defining Catholic doctrine so that no one was in any doubt about how to worship and the doctrine to follow. The 25 articles of faith became law in 1543. In 1544 a **list of condemned books** was published.

John Calvin (see page 16) was slowly emerging as the main influence in French Protestantism, reinforced by the publication of his *Institutes* in French in 1541. The first edition had been dedicated to Francis, evidence perhaps that Calvin believed the King sympathetic towards reform, and also a statement to his co-reformers and supporters in his native France that French Protestants were not the rebels that they were being made out to be. The *Institutes* were banned one year later, and a heretic in Rouen was burned at the stake for quoting from them. As evidence of heresy increased, Francis became more active in his repression. Heretical ideas and doctrine permeated French society in the 1540s and the number of heresy cases brought before the *parlement* of Paris increased because of this growth and the increasing vigilance of the authorities.

CONCLUSION: FRANCIS I AND RELIGION

- Francis took a consistently hard line on heresy, and while sympathetic towards the moderate reform of Lefèvre and willing to patronise humanists at court, he never tolerated attacks on Catholic doctrine.
- The Affair of the Placards clarified the religious problem for Francis and defined the line between humanism and heresy. Francis inevitably became more active in promoting persecution as the threat from heresy increased.
- Protestantism made little headway in France during the 1520s and early 1530s but under the influence of Calvin made real progress in the 1540s.
- Francis was reluctant to cede power to the Sorbonne and the *parlement*s in the 1530s but he was forced to recognise the growing threat of Protestantism in French society in the 1540s and give these institutions more authority to search, arrest and try heretics.
- Heresy and attacks on Catholicism fundamentally undermined the rule of the French king, as his authority was based on the will of God and the one true faith. Francis had to uphold his image as the Most Christian King and heretics were seen as seditious and dangerous rebels who contaminated society. They had to be eradicated.

DOMESTIC POLICY

The primary issue concerning the domestic policies of Francis I appears to be the extent to which he was able to centralise French government and lay the foundations for absolutism. The ability of Francis to collect taxation and maintain law and order effectively is a marker as to how strong and centralised his royal authority became between 1515 and 1547:

- Francis never felt vulnerable or weak enough to summon the Estates General (see page 20) and only in 1527 did he call an **Assembly of Notables** which comprised leading clerics, nobles and *parlementaires*. The assembly therefore acted as an extension of the king's council and was summoned, and to a great extent controlled, by the king himself.
- Taxation demands were high throughout the reign of Francis I, but there was a surprising lack of resistance from the third estate (see page 23) in the face of such fiscal pressure.
- Outbreaks of popular revolt were few, although a serious revolt did occur in western France in 1542. In response to the king's attempts to reform the *gabelle*, salt tax, through the Edict of Chatellerault, the people of the salt marshes took up arms. In 1542, over 10,000 men took advantage of the king's absence fighting Charles V to force the royal commissioners out of the localities. Only the personal intervention of Francis I quashed the revolt and the king himself arrived at La Rochelle to pass judgement on the rebels. In the end they were pardoned, although they were made to deliver a quantity of salt to the royal warehouse in Rouen, which was subsequently used to pay off debts. Francis did ultimately get his way over the reform of the salt tax two years later.
- More typical of his attitude towards dissenters was perhaps the manner in which he ordered the town of Lagny-sur-Marne to be sacked in 1544 following revolt over the *gabelle*.

What was the nature of Francis I's relationship with the nobility?

Given the strong personal nature of Francis I's rule it is

Francis I at a meeting of the parlement.

unsurprising that there were few noble revolts over the course of his reign. In the main the old nobility remained loyal to the crown and helped to implement royal policy in the localities. One exception exists in the form of Charles of Bourbon, which tells us that even in periods of strong monarchy, the nobility remained a potential threat to the authority of the crown.

The Bourbon Rebellion, 1523

- Charles of Bourbon was the most powerful nobleman in France. He had vast land holdings in central France, and within his territories he exerted enormous political power. Indeed to many of his subjects he was as powerful as a king. He levied taxes, made laws and raised armies. Additionally Bourbon held the position of Constable of France, which gave him control of the king's armies during peacetime, and during war he would lead the royal army were the king absent.
- Relations between the King and Bourbon were relatively cordial until Bourbon's wife, Suzanne, died in April 1521. Her will left all of her land to her husband, a decision that was contested by Francis I's mother Louise of Savoy. The original marriage between Charles and

Suzanne had reunited the Bourbon house and brought together all landholdings. Now on the death of Suzanne with no male issue, it was inevitable that the crown would lay claim to territories which had once belonged to them.

- Louise was Suzanne's first cousin and nearest blood relative. Francis also laid claim to Bourbon land because there was no male issue from the marriage. *Parlement* ordered that the Bourbon demesne be dismantled and land claimed by the crown be handed over.

- Disgruntled and embittered, Charles of Bourbon **looked abroad for support**. In 1522 he concluded an alliance with Emperor Charles V and Henry VIII which outlined an invasion of France from both north and south to reclaim lost lands. By this treaty Bourbon would also marry one of Charles V's sisters. The plot was uncovered but this did not prevent an English invasion of Picardy in September 1522 which resulted in an English army getting to within 50 miles of Paris. Bourbon's planned invasion of Franche Comte did not receive the imperial aid which had been promised and thus fell through. Bourbon was stripped of his offices and fled into Italy in 1523.

- In 1524 another treaty was concluded between Henry VIII and Charles V in which each agreed to contribute 100,000 crowns towards an invasion of France led by Bourbon. In July Bourbon led an imperial army into Provence and quickly captured the capital of Aix on 9 August. Bourbon now ordered his men to lay siege to Marseilles, but the town held out. As the royal army approached Avignon, Bourbon retreated.

- Bourbon continued to serve in the imperial army in northern Italy, leading his men towards Rome in 1527. The city was brutally sacked in one of the most infamous events of the sixteenth century. Bourbon died there. In France, Bourbon's associates and accomplices were arrested whilst his lands passed over to the crown.

KEY THEMES

Looked abroad for support Any noble rebellion was a threat to the authority of the crown. The Bourbon rebellion was particularly troublesome because it involved powerful foreign elements. The fact that Bourbon was able to lay seige to Marseilles demonstrates the seriousness of the rebellion for Francis. The fact that Francis was able to repel Bourbon and ultimately confiscate his lands demonstrates his strength as a ruler. Later in the period, in the 1580s, Henry III was powerless to prevent Spanish intervention on behalf of militant Catholic nobles; actions which severely undermine the authority of the crown.

What can Francis I's dealings with the parlement of Rouen tell us about his power?

In many ways the *parlements* were the most significant guarantors of provincial liberties and privilege, and their twin roles of acting as courts of law and ratifying royal legislation made them potentially important checks on royal authority. Francis believed that the *parlement* should automatically pass royal laws, but he knew that they could stand in the way of his increasing demands for taxation or the creation of more royal offices for sale. In 1539, Francis vented his anger towards the provincial *parlement* of Rouen:

- The *parlement* at Rouen delayed the passing of an important law, the Ordinance of Villers-Cotterêts. When it was eventually passed in 1540 it left out the points which it found unacceptable. Francis told the *parlement* that he was preparing to travel to Rouen and sort out the problem personally. He went to Rouen, closed the court down and took the seals.
- Some of the Rouen magistrates whom Francis believed were loyal, stayed on to judge criminal cases in Normandy and others held Grand Jours in Bayeaux which served as a travelling court of session to try criminal cases throughout the province. The *parlement* of Rouen was reopened in 1541 after Francis was satisfied with the loyalty of its members and the work of the Grand Jours.

How far did Francis override the liberties of the provincial estates?

Provincial estates continued to operate along traditional lines, and in theory they were representative of provincial rights. Yet the estates were not democratic and the king decided where and when they met as well as fixing the agenda and choosing the president.

- The estates had the right to make complaints to the king through royal commissioners and in theory their requests were supposed to be addressed before any form of taxation or subsidy was granted to the crown.
- However, Francis often ran roughshod over such provincial rights, especially when he urgently needed a subsidy to finance the Italian Wars. In 1538, Francis told his commissioners at Albi to take the subsidy first and hear the grievances later.

- In 1537, the *gabelle* was extended to Languedoc and then Normandy in 1546 despite the fact that both were exempt from the salt tax.
- Fiscal pressures increased and Francis often imposed his will at the expense of local rights and privileges. Yet Francis still needed the support of central government and local institutions to maintain law and order and run the country. At a local level, Francis still relied upon his **provincial governors**, and *baillis* (see page 21). Leading nobles fulfilled the roles of provincial governors and acted as local representatives of central authority.

How far did France develop as a nation state under Francis I?

France made some important steps towards becoming a nation state under Francis I, although it was never his primary intention to promote nationhood. Francis I's main priority was to advance his own authority and any other developments were a by-product of this central aim.

Still, the incorporation of Brittany in 1532 followed by the Edict of Villers Cotterets (1539) served to lay the foundations of a nation state. Brittany helped to shape France into the modern hexagon we recognise today. Yet, as with any newly acquired territory it would take time to assimilate the province into the kingdom of France. Often this process was made more difficult by provincial liberties and customs which the crown could not erode. Territories such as Brittany were often exempt from certain royal taxes, employed their own laws and spoke their own language.

The Edict of Villers Cotterets was primarily intended to reform the judicial system, but it also decreed that all legal documents in the kingdom were to be written in French. From this time, records of baptisms, marriages and deaths were to be in French. Yet the shift away from Latin in legal circles did not necessarily mean the advent of a uniform French language. *Langue d'oil* was the official language of court and it made some progress southwards eroding *langue d'oc* on the way, but by no means was *langue d'oil* spoken or used throughout France by the end of the early modern period. Local dialects and different languages continued to exist. Indeed even in the reign of Francis I there were five principal languages spoken – French, Occitan, Basque, Breton and Flemish as well as countless dialects. Academics and the educated elite did start to write in French and works such as Joachim du Bellay's *Defence and Illustration of the French Language* (1549) championed French over Latin. Occasionally the use of French was forced upon newly acquired territories such as Metz in the 1550s in order to create a sense of linguistic community and inspire loyalty to the French crown.

Therefore, in the long term Francis I may have done his bit to promote a nation state, but France was still some way off territorial, legal and linguistic unity. Still in 1526, the Estates of Burgundy remained loyal to the French crown in the wake of Francis I's capture at Pavia. Overtures were made to Burgundy by the Holy Roman Empire and at a time of crisis for the French crown after the Battle of Pavia such a move to the Empire may have been attractive. Yet the loyalty of Burgundy perhaps demonstrates that Francis I had engendered a sense of belonging amongst the newly acquired provinces.

To what extent did royal bureaucracy increase under Francis I?

In terms of central government, Francis ruled through the king's council and it was in his reign that the *conseil des affaires* developed into an important decision-making body. Moreover royal bureaucracy also increased with one royal administrator existing for every 60 square kilometres in 1515, and growing to one for every 45 by 1547. Francis came increasingly to rely upon the *maîtres des requêtes de l'hôtel* who were officials trained in the law who worked in the chancery and served as a link between various departments of state. Such men were ennobled for their efforts, and one might argue that their increased responsibility and the complex nature of royal government served to sideline the aristocracy.

Why was venality becoming increasingly important to French kings?

Francis knowingly created more offices and sold them to increase revenue, a practice known as venality. The short-term financial rewards for Francis were substantial, and, while the major councillors of the realm remained princes of the blood and leading nobles, the systematic creation and sale of offices did create a new noble class, the nobility of the robe, who over time challenged the political power of the old nobility. The number of offices or government posts rose from 4,000 in 1515 to over 46,000 in 1665: there is little doubt that this trend began under Francis I.

The market for offices was huge, with many seeing their purchase as a way of improving their social standing. Yet such practice did create problems for Francis and his successors:

- Important royal offices tended to become the property of a small group of families although Francis did try to counter this with the 40-day rule which declared resignations invalid unless the owner survived 40 days after making the act of resignation. The penalty was forfeiture of the office back to the crown, and so anyone dying on the job produced a windfall for the king's coffers. On the whole, however, offices were often handed down to relatives or friends.
- In an attempt to increase revenue, offices were often divided into two or three thus creating more layers of bureaucracy and in the long run creating more salaries to be paid.
- While venality often meant that the king could choose his office holders carefully and expect loyalty from them, it also created a political power base which in some ways diluted the king's authority and power. Certainly a king who had aspirations of absolutism should not have to depend upon venality for fiscal security.

Trends in domestic policy

While there were few innovations in the reign of Francis I with regard to administration we do see a number of trends developing:

- Royal government was becoming increasingly centralised through the effective use of provincial governors, *baillis* and *maîtres des requêtes de l'hôtel*. Royal control over the provinces was increasing.

- Although royal legislation was still subject to the ratification of the *parlement* and taxation was in theory granted by provincial estates, the king's will often trampled on local traditions and privileges.
- Popular resistance to royal policy under Francis I was rare and easily subdued.
- Through the systematic use of venality more royal offices were created. Financial rewards must be balanced against the long-term problems of hereditary offices and reliance upon such practice.
- A by-product of venality was the creation of a new noble class, the nobility of the robe, and it could be argued that Francis began to sideline the old nobility and relied more upon trained professionals who specialised in certain areas of royal administration.
- Limitations on royal authority continued to exist. The *parlement* still had to ratify legislation; provincial estates had to grant subsidies; tax collection was haphazard; and maintaining law and order in the frontier regions was still a problem.
- Francis was not an absolutist monarch, but he did bring a greater sense of centralisation and uniformity to French government and ultimately his word held sway over provincial liberties.

THE ARTS AND ARCHITECTURE

Francis I's court

Artistic styles and architecture were used by Francis to reflect not only the enlightened nature of his kingship but also the power of his authority and the grandeur of his monarchy. To begin with the court of Francis I was much larger than that of his predecessors. The court was generally made up of the **royal household** and nobles who were eager to attain the king's ear and his patronage. The size of the royal court had been on the increase since the early fifteenth century, and by 1535 Francis employed over 600 household officials on a permanent basis. The actual size of the court was much greater, totalling nearly 10,000 people depending upon its location and the political circumstances.

Royal household Attended to the needs of the king, through three main departments. The chapel met the king's spiritual needs; the chamber ran the day-to-day affairs of the king's bedchamber; the hotel fed the court.

How important was the court to the image of Francis I?

Importantly, the court was **nomadic**, which allowed the king to undertake relatively frequent royal progresses to visit the outlying provinces. Thus the king's subjects saw their monarch while Francis also used such opportunities to patronise local nobles and allow them to join the court. In short, the nomadic nature of the court contributed to the centralisation of royal authority. The makeup of the court under Francis also reflected his Renaissance aspirations in that more Italians were present in the royal entourage. Primarily this came about because Francis was looking to attain further political influence and potential military allies south of the Alps, and often Italian princes looked to Francis for protection from Habsburg oppression. Moreover, the marriage of Henry of Orleans, second son of Francis, to Catherine de Medici in 1533 brought a significant number of Florentines to the French court. Frenchmen also served in Italian courts and the consequence of such interaction was that a greater refinement and extravagance was brought to the French court in terms of the arts and literature. Clothes, entertainment, food, dress and jewels were all supposed to demonstrate the grandeur and status of the court and the monarch.

The Visual arts

In painting and sculpture Francis employed a number of Italian artists. Early in his reign after the conquest of Milan in 1515, he invited **Leonardo da Vinci** to France, and slightly later Andrea del Sarto. Both enjoyed the King's patronage and company and there is little doubt that Francis was an enthusiastic and knowledgeable patron of the arts. Later, in 1531, Rosso's art and in particular his murals characterised Fontainebleau. Francis also collected art, avidly acquiring work by the artists Raphael and Aretino. **Benvenuto Cellini** visited France in 1537 and 1540, producing a silver statue of Jupiter for the King and a bronze relief of the Nymph of Fontainebleau. Non-Italian painters of note were Jean Clouet and his son François, both leading portrait painters. Although born in the Netherlands, Jean Clouet was trained in France and his portraits of the King and his family were much admired.

Chateau de Blois.

Had a workshop in the Petit Nesle opposite the Louvre, and he was well rewarded for his work. Yet his arrogant and aloof manner made him many enemies and he was frequently attacked or verbally abused in public. Despite this, Cellini's second stay in Paris lasted for five years and his autobiography as well as his art leaves us with a lasting impression of the court of Francis I.

Ordinance of Montpellier Law which required all printers and booksellers to deliver a copy of every new book to the royal librarian at Blois.

Francis was also regarded as a great patron of humanism, a fact reinforced by the establishment of four royal lectureships in Greek and Hebrew in 1530. Although their significance has perhaps been overestimated by some who would like to see the *lecteurs royaux* as a symbol of the King's support of the humanists against the conservative Sorbonne, they were still an indication of the enlightened nature of Francis I. The King was also noted as a keen collector of literature, as the libraries at Blois and Fontainebleau bear witness. In 1537, the King even passed the **Ordinance of Montpellier**. Poetry and literature played an important role in the sixteenth century as forms of propaganda, glorifying military victories and reinforcing the power and authority of the crown. The foremost court poet was Clement Marot, whose career was disrupted by the fact that he held evangelical sympathies which forced him into exile. The leading literary figure of the period in France was François Rabelais whose chronicles were typical of his satirical humour which amused the King and offended the authorities, most notably the Sorbonne.

CHAPTER SUMMARY: WHAT ASPECTS OF CONTINUITY CAN WE SEE BETWEEN LOUIS XII AND FRANCIS I?

- Both are perceived as Renaissance monarchs who were interested in good government. Francis was more extravagant in terms of patronage, court life and overall expenditure.
- The scale and expense of wars in Italy increased under Francis and therefore the impact on the economy is greater. Still the rationale for war remained the same.
- Both looked to increase royal revenue but again Francis was forced to do so on a larger scale. Similarly, both sought to make royal government more efficient, integrate new provinces and erode particularism. Both had limited success.
- Both were interested in the concept of Church reform but again in reality achieved little. By the end of Francis I's reign, Protestantism was beginning to appear in France. Although it made little headway initially,

Protestantism was a challenge to the authority of the crown as well as that of the Catholic Church.

- Both monarchs benefitted from a period of long, stable rule and economic prosperity.
- Louis was more willing to rule with the advice of *parlement*, leading to claims that Francis was authoritarian in his manner of rule.
- Neither faced much in the way of noble rebellion, and when faction did arise they were both powerful enough to control it in the interests of the crown.

The specification key themes across the period can be summarised as follows:

Nation state

The actions of Francis I in eroding provincial liberties are not necessarily those of a monarch interested in furthering the notion of a nation state. It is more likely that the centralisation of government was aimed at increasing royal authority and increasing revenue from the localities. The Concordat of Bologna should be seen in the same light. Whilst creating the foundations of a French national Church, the real reason for this development was to increase the authority of the crown in clerical affairs.

Relations between kings and subjects

Government remained unrepresentative of the people, a point highlighted by the fact that Francis never summoned an Estates General. Taxation demands increased due to the Italian Wars, and such actions could create popular discontent (see below). The Bourbon Rebellion in 1523 makes clear that even in times of strong Renaissance kingship, the nobility remained a potential threat.

Religious developments

For the first time in this period, we can see the divisions and problems created by the emergence of heterodox opinion. By the end of Francis I's reign Protestantism was beginning to make ground in France, despite royal persecution. Catholic unity was under threat, and this trend intensified over the next two decades, weakening the crown and leading the nation into civil war.

Social and economic developments

Growing taxation demands moved the third estate in western France to violent rebellion in 1542. With no political representation and little means of voicing protest, the only way for the Third Estate to show their displeasure was to resort to arms. Of course, such actions rarely changed royal policy, and any popular disturbances were dealt with harshly. At a social level, Francis I's growing reliance upon venality created more office holders and the relatively prosperous economic climate allowed for some social mobility.

QUESTIONS TO CONSIDER

1. In what respects did the Affair of the Placards mark a turning point in the religious outlook of Francis I?

2. Was Francis I consultative in his domestic policies or authoritarian?

3. How serious was the threat posed by the Bourbon rebellion?

4. In what ways did Francis fulfil the characteristics of a Renaissance monarch?

CHAPTER 4

Henry II and the origins of the French Wars of Religion

THE NEW KING

What were the changes made at court under Henry II?

Immediately after the death of Francis I and coronation of Henry II, there was an inevitable court reshuffle as Francis's favourites were replaced by those close to Henry, especially **Diane de Poitiers**:

- Also returning to court and favour was Anne de Montmorency who had fallen from power in 1541. Restored in 1547 as president of the king's council, four years later he was made a duke.
- One noble family of great importance which also benefited from Henry's patronage was the Guise family, especially Francis and Charles, sons of Claude, Duke of Guise. Soon Charles, already Archbishop of Reims, was made a cardinal and his brother a duke. Their five brothers and four sisters all married into influential families, most notably Mary who had married James V of Scotland in 1538 with whom she had a daughter, the future Mary, Queen of Scots.

Diane de Poitiers, mistress of Henry II, portrayed as the Roman goddess of the hunt.

Historians have tended to ignore the reign of Henry II because it was short and nondescript in comparison to that of his father. Yet, despite not having the intellect of Francis, Henry coped well with the strains of royal government and there is much to suggest that he was a serious and conscientious ruler who continued to project the glory and power of the crown through foreign affairs, art and architecture.

Henry and the provinces Henry was just as capable of enforcing royal authority at the expense of the provinces as Francis had been. In June 1549, Henry was granted a supplement to the *taille*, known as the *taillon*, by the estates of Normandy to pay for the French army garrisoned there and relieve some of the pressures associated with billeting from the local populace. Henry continued to collect the *taillon* for years afterwards and still billeted troops in Normandy.

KEY EVENTS

Violence in Bordeaux This was particularly acute: a leading royal official was lynched and salt tax collectors murdered and their bodies covered in salt. In October, Henry sent Montmorency and Aumale to Bordeaux with 10,000 troops to put down the revolt. The *parlement* was dissolved and the authorities were punished for failing to subdue the rebellion and maintain order. The city was stripped of its privileges and fined accordingly. Over 150 rebels were executed in Bordeaux.

DOMESTIC POLICY AND ADMINISTRATION

How far did Henry II centralise the French Government?

Like Francis, Henry continued to centralise French government and erode the **liberties of the provinces** whenever possible: neither king called an Estates General. Thus, as with Francis, the consent of the provincial estates often came second to the King's interests:

- In terms of centralisation Henry passed an important piece of legislation in 1552 which created a new law court called the *siège présidial* to judge certain criminal and civil cases. Sixty of these courts were put into operation; they were overseen by two lieutenants, seven councillors and, from 1557, a president and a chancery.
- *Bailliages* tended to be absorbed into *présidiaux* and such courts tended to judge local land disputes, acting as an appeal court on property under the value of 250 livres. In some ways they increased royal authority in the localities and brought uniformity in lesser provincial land cases, but their real worth to the king was the creation of further new offices which could be sold for profit. In this respect, Henry carried on the trend established by his father.
- In a similar respect to Francis I, Henry II faced little popular opposition to his rule, although there was the continuing issue of the *gabelle* (salt tax), which Francis had attempted to reform in 1542, a policy which met with resistance in western France. In 1548, Henry II ordered the policy for a single salt tax levied at the salt marsh and a system of royal warehouses. Once more trouble ensued in the west, particularly in Angoumois, Perigord and Saintonge where over 20,000 rebels took up arms against tax officials, destroying warehouses and murdering royal commissioners. The revolt grew in size throughout August 1548 spreading to **Bordeaux** and Cognac. Soon the rebels began targeting the homes of the rich and the nature of the uprising became more generally based on class. After the uprising had been crushed, Henry was wise enough to recognise what had caused the problem in the first place and by 1553 the salt tax had been abolished in the west and an amnesty offered to the rebels.

How effective were Henry II's financial policies?

Financially there were few innovations during the reign of Henry II, and generally he subjected the third estate to the same fiscal pressures as his father had done in order to finance foreign affairs.

- The *taillon* served to support the military in 1549, while in 1552 a new clerical tax raised an additional 1.4 million livres per annum.
- Traditional sources of revenue were tapped, but initially with greater success. In his first year, Henry collected 8.4 million livres from taxation, an increase of 25 per cent on his father's haul in 1515. Such an increase may well be an indication of the extent to which father and son had managed to bring some uniformity and centralisation to fiscal machinery.
- Venality continued to be a short-term money spinner for the crown aided not only by the presidial courts but also by the formation of a new *parlement* at Rennes in 1552.
- Like his father, Henry relied on bankers' loans to subsidise his foreign policy, borrowing 1.2 million livres from the Lyons bankers in 1552 and a further 1.8 million a year later. Francis had pursued a similar policy, but Henry was able to gain a favourable credit rating with the bankers of Lyons because he instituted a systematic way of repaying debt.
- In 1555, he introduced the *grand parti de Lyons* (a special treasury) which promised four annual repayments, instilling a confidence among the bankers which allowed Henry to negotiate further loans amounting to over 10 million livres in 1555–56.

Yet ultimately Henry's legacy, like his father's, was one of debt and fiscal insecurity.

CONCLUSION: HOW POWERFUL WERE THE RENAISSANCE MONARCHS – LOUIS XII, FRANCIS I AND HENRY II?

Now that we have covered the domestic policies of three monarchs it is time to compare and contrast these reigns and identify themes and trends across the period 1498–1559.

Renaissance monarchy

Historians tend to characterise Louis XII, Francis I and Henry II as Renaissance monarchs. Glenn Richardson (*History Review*, September 1998) argues that the transition between medieval king and Renaissance prince can be seen with Louis XII (1462–1515). On the one hand, Louis XII might be regarded as a Renaissance monarch in the way that he began centralising government, codifying the legal system and controlling the power of the nobility; but on the other, he might be seen as a medieval prince in the sense that few of his reforms could really be labelled innovative. Richardson cites the example of the Ordinance of Blois (1499) as a piece of legislation that came out of meetings with the Estates General and Assembly of Notables – not a tool to curb noble power but a royal directive to improve the judicial system that was acknowledged by the nobility in return for recognition of their status by the crown.

The changing character of the nobility

In *A History of France, 1460–1560* (Macmillan, 1995), David Potter picks up on a central theme that runs throughout this period: the rise of the nobility of the robe. Traditionally, the rise of this new administrative class of nobility has been viewed as being at the expense of the old nobility of the sword. In short, the crown deliberately sold offices and created the new nobility in order to weaken the old magnates who continually posed a threat to the monarchy. Potter, Mack Holt (*Society and Institutions in Early Modern France*, University of Georgia, 1991) and Philip Hoffman have done much to add caution to this argument. Certainly a new noble class did emerge in the sixteenth century and venality was a constant means of increasing the royal income. Yet, although major noble families such as Guise and Montmorency were not as powerfully independent of the crown as they had been in the fifteenth century, nor were they excluded from power. Holt and Potter emphasise that the old nobility retained their social prominence throughout the sixteenth century, and during the Italian Wars played a critical role in raising and leading armies for the king. Moreover, while the new nobility undoubtedly attained greater political influence, not all received offices that led to an increase in power or got them closer to the king. In *The Nobility of the Election of Bayeaux, 1463–1666* (Princeton, 1980), J. B. Wood has demonstrated in his study of Bayeaux that the nobility of the sword and the nobility of the robe were almost indistinguishable rather than being two separate groups. Some old nobility held offices just like the new, while some new nobility lived nobly as one would expect the old to. The key to understanding the fate of the nobility in sixteenth-century France, according to Wood, was not old or new nobility but rich or poor nobility and the general trend in Bayeaux was towards a richer noble class.

Was the power of the nobility declining?

The traditional line fostered by historians writing in the first half of the twentieth century was that of a nobility in crisis. The economic decline of the nobility went hand in hand with their political and social fall from power at the expense of the crown. Lucien Romier (1922), Gaston Roupnel (1955) and Paul Raveau (1926) undertook local case-studies that shaped our view of the nobility in France during this period. The trends appeared to be the same, that of an economic boom in the first half of the sixteenth century that gave way to depression and consequently noble decline. Noble landowners made good in the 1520s and 1530s when labour was cheap, harvests good and land plentiful; and suffered ruin in the 1570s and 1580s when inflation was high, rents fixed, harvests poor and civil war rampant. Yet Wood, Holt and J. M. Constant ('Nobles et paysans beaucerons aux XVIe at XVIIe siècles', thesis, Lille, 1981) have shown such a portrayal to be false. Both Constant and Holt have demonstrated that many of the very wealthy nobility made a profit out of the Wars of Religion and, far from selling land, many nobles actually bought it during the Wars of Religion. While some lesser nobles went under, and perhaps those who had begun to live nobly at the start of the sixteenth century slipped back into the third estate, the main core of the nobility survived and thrived. As R. J. Knecht writes in *The Rise and Fall of Renaissance France 1483–1610*, Blackwell, 2001:

> *The traditional view of aristocratic decline rested on three assumptions: first, that siegneural rents were fixed and paid in money; secondly that war helped to ruin the*

nobility; and thirdly that extravagant living and a lack of business sense contributed to that ruin. All three are questionable. The king continued to rely upon the old nobility in the provinces and court did not attract the number of nobles that was once thought.

Richardson agrees:

the two groups (old and new nobility) formed an expanded oligarchy which was prepared to deal with the monarchy in order to secure for itself the lucrative pensions, positions in the royal household and the myriad of offices in the localities.

Therefore, there has been a significant reappraisal of the role of the nobility within French society over the past two decades. The picture of a nobility in crisis has given way to one in which the old aristocracy actually suffered little change and in many senses benefited from the chaos and turmoil of the sixteenth century.

Can we describe the Renaissance monarchs as absolute?

Another major point of debate among historians is the extent to which the authority of the crown increased during this period, reaching its zenith under Louis XIV. The nature of Renaissance kingship under Francis I and Henry II, and in particular the extent of the limitations on their authority, remain contentious points. Were the Valois monarchs paving the way for Bourbon absolutism? George Pagès believes that Francis and Henry were absolutist, with few obstacles to their outright authority. Yet other historians, such as Henri Prentout and J. Russell Major (*Representative Institutions in Renaissance France, 1421–1559*, Madison, 1960) are cautious about such an outright endorsement of absolutism, drawing attention to the rights and privileges of the *pays d'états* alongside the decentralised political structure within France that naturally curbed royal authority. Russell Major sees the reign of Francis I as popular and consultative rather than absolutist. He points to dealings with the *parlements* and the way in which Francis consulted his subjects over foreign policy as evidence of a monarch prepared to seek advice and consent before embarking upon important policy decisions. Yet

Knecht takes issue with Russell Major, demonstrating that in many ways Francis's reign had the hallmarks of an absolutist monarchy: for example, the way in which the Concordat of Bologna was forced through *parlements* despite impinging upon clerical Gallicanism, or the way in which Francis treated the provincial *parlements*, most notably that in Rouen. Moreover, neither Francis nor Henry ever called a meeting of the Estates General and an assembly of notables was called in 1527 only to raise a large subsidy to pay the ransom of Henry's two sons held captive in Madrid. Knecht points out that even when provincial estates were asked to ratify a treaty the decision had already been taken by the king's council: the deputies were simply rubber-stamping the decree. The way in which the king pardoned the salt tax rebels of 1542 at La Rochelle has also been put forward as an example of how Francis treated his subjects with compassion and magnanimity. Yet, as Knecht points out, the *gabelle* was not scrapped and in the midst of a war with the emperor, troops could not be freed to deal with the 10,000 armed rebels. Francis had no option but to be conciliatory.

Therefore, historians debate the extent to which Renaissance monarchy was absolute, that is without subordination to any other human authority or institution; or contractual, that is answerable to institutions and expected to consult with them on major issues of state. The reality probably lay somewhere in between. Provincial liberties and *parlements* continued to prove an obstacle to royal authority. Less so in the long and stable reign of Francis I admittedly, but they became more politically prominent in the second half of the sixteenth century. Law and order in the localities was erratic even in the reign of Francis and political power so decentralised that to use the term absolutist would be false. Yet, on the other hand, the image of a benevolent, caring and contractual monarch has to be treated with caution. Francis rode roughshod over provincial liberties whenever he could, pandering to them only when he needed money. No consultative institution had the chance even to meet during the reigns of Francis or Henry! Therefore, in the context of the sixteenth century, the reigns of the Renaissance monarchs were closer to Knecht's authoritarianism than Russell Major's consultation.

RELIGION UNDER HENRY II

Why were relations between Henry II and the Papacy strained?

Henry followed a harsh policy of repression towards French Protestants but also relations between the monarchy and the papacy were strained because of:

- the papal alliance with Charles V in the war over Parma
- the decision of Pope Julius III to reconvene the General Council to the Imperial city of Trent.

Henry rightly concluded that papal sympathies now lay with the emperor so he ordered all French bishops away from the council, cutting the payment of annates to Rome (the payments made by clerics on their appointment to benefices) and proposing the establishment of a French council as a national alternative to the **Council of Trent**. Julius threatened to excommunicate Henry II, while the latter hinted that a complete break with Rome was imminent. With relations at their worst, a compromise was found and an agreement made between Henry and Julius in 1552:

- Henry promised not to call a Gallican council.
- Julius in return allowed Henry to continue collecting annates.

Ultimately, Henry was unwilling to go the same way as Henry VIII of England and break with Rome. He realised how important his role was as guardian of the Church and how unpopular a split with Rome would be among French conservatives in the Sorbonne. Julius too, saw how damaging a split with France would be to the Catholic cause just as the General Council was attempting to address the second wave of Protestant reform. The whole episode demonstrates that Henry was willing to protect Gallican interests against Rome, and fulfil his duties as protector of the French Church.

How did Henry II attempt to combat the growth of heresy?

Henry was steadfastly orthodox and conservative in his

KEY EVENTS

Council of Trent Henry was not interested in a General Council which was working towards a resolution of the religious policies of the Holy Roman Empire. The spread of heresy had weakened the emperor throughout the first half of the sixteenth century, and had largely worked in France's favour during the Habsburg–Valois struggle.

religious outlook, a fact reflected in the creation of the *chambre ardente* (burning chamber) in 1547. Henry followed up the creation of the *chambre ardente* with the Edict of Châteaubriand in 1551:

- The edict banned the printing, sale or possession of Protestant literature while also prohibiting any gatherings or secret assemblies of heretics.
- Rewards and incentives were offered for informers who would receive one-third of the confiscated property of anyone they named who was successfully prosecuted for heresy.
- Magistrates were also given the right to actively search out Protestants, raiding homes of suspected heretics or those in which they might be sheltered. Interestingly, the edict made little reference to Calvinism, instead still incorrectly talking of the Lutheran heresy, yet the message of the legislation was a clear one. Heretics were dangerous and seditious rebels, who undermined the natural social order and hierarchy. Even the magistrates of the *parlements* were to be examined every three months in order to ensure their dogmatic orthodoxy.

Yet Henry was distracted during this period by events elsewhere, most notably in Italy. While he was preoccupied, heresy continued to progress. Indeed, Calvinism was not just finding support among the artisans and lower classes, as the king himself believed, but it was finding favour among some of the nobility.

How was Calvinism able to expand in the face of harsh persecution?

As the French crown was devising means to destroy heresy, so John Calvin, Pierre Viret and Guillaume Farel were promoting their doctrine from Geneva. Calvin's **French Institutes** (1541) had made a huge impact, and were accordingly banned by the authorities in 1542. Calvin's works also featured prominently on the list of prohibited books drawn up in 1544, yet the amount of Calvinist literature and propaganda arriving from abroad continued to increase. The Edict of Châteaubriand created more French exiles who settled in Geneva, creating a base from which further literature and strategies emerged to galvanise

Urban-based Calvinism
Trial records tend to show a disproportionate number of the clergy and urban elites indicted for heresy and these are the social groups which we would normally associate with Calvinism. The fact that the majority of missionaries were sent to urban centres such as Poitiers or Orleans reinforces this point.

the reformed cause in France. The success of **urban-based Calvinism** in France during the 1550s and 1560s can be attributed to many factors:

- Geneva was geographically close to the French trade centre of Lyons, and much literature was smuggled into France and disseminated throughout the kingdom via Lyons.
- Calvin was French, and he took a special interest in the progress of the reform movement in his homeland. He still had an extensive network of contacts and friends within the kingdom and, with no figure emerging to lead the movement from within France, Calvin established himself as the natural figurehead for French Protestants.
- Calvin himself was very active in terms of writing polemics which attacked the Catholic Church and offered guidance for his co-religionaries in France. Works such as *Little Treatise on the Lord's Supper*, *What a Faithful Man should do among the Papists* and *Apology to the Nicodemites* all contributed to the success of the movement.
- Small, secret underground groups called conventicles (which sprang up during the 1520s) were spiritually nourished by the works of Calvin emanating from Geneva during the 1540s. For the first time, those who did not conform to Catholicism were given direction and advice.
- During times of harsh repression, Calvin's letters to those under persecution offered solace and a sense of belonging. Calvin tied his French contacts closely to his church in Geneva, and the increasing number of refugees in that city also strengthened the bond with France. In time Calvin would oversee the training of ministers and pastors in Geneva and send them back to France as Calvinist missionaries. Of the 88 missionaries sent to France between 1555 and 1562, 62 were French by birth. After the establishment of the Genevan Academy in 1559, under Theodore de Beza, the number of missionaries increased.

Why did Calvinism attract support from the French nobility?

Calvinism's success in France came from the support not only of the artisans but also of the nobility who offered the movement protection, finance and status. The period 1555–62 witnessed the recruitment of influential nobles in Guyenne, Gascony, Normandy, Dauphine and Languedoc. Calvin deliberately targeted the nobility, knowing the benefits of their support. Noble missionaries were sent back to France well versed in the gospel and the organisation of the Calvinist Church.

- Several leading members of the Bourbon family, themselves princes of the blood, were early converts, among them Antoine de Bourbon, **King of Navarre**, who had vast holdings in the south-west around Gascony and Guyenne. Calvin set up a personal correspondence with Navarre and it is no surprise that the earliest Calvinist congregations emerged in the relative security of the south-west.
- Other leading **noble converts** in this period were Louis de Bourbon, Prince of Condé, the younger brother of Antoine who had actually visited Geneva in person in 1555. Condé played a crucial role as the military leader of the Huguenots during the initial years of the Wars of Religion.
- The Châtillon family also provided noble converts, most notably Gaspard de Coligny who owned much land in Normandy. He and his two brothers became fervent supporters of Calvin despite the fact that they were nephews of Anne de Montmorency, the Constable of France (France's military leader). Other lesser nobles converted for political or personal gain, but during the 1550s as Calvinism sought to extend its feelers throughout France it mattered not. Noble support enabled Calvinism to spread from the cities into the countryside, and congregations could worship in relative safety on the estates of the nobility.

How strong was the Calvinist movement by 1559?

Throughout the 1550s French Calvinists became not only more numerous but also better organised and more unified:

KEY THEMES

Navarre and Calvinism
Antoine de Bourbon, King of Navarre, was never fully committed to the cause, unlike his wife Jeanne d'Albret, herself the daughter of Francis I's sister Marguerite who had been such a leading supporter of the Circle of Meaux. Navarre's son Henry became the military and political leader of the Huguenot cause before returning to Catholicism in 1593 in order to become king of France.

The nobility and Calvinism For Coligny and Louis de Bourbon, the attraction of the new faith was theological and in that respect genuine. In short, they were committed adherents of the gospel and believed in Calvin's view of the eucharist.

More than 100 people were arrested and three were consequently burned in the Place Maubert. Worse still, Catholic propaganda purported that the congregation was taking part in lewd sexual acts, material which did the movement no favours.

KEY THEMES

Calvinism at a local level
A whole network of provincial synods, consistories and colloquies existed throughout France; it bound local churches and provinces together.

KEY PEOPLE

Anne du Bourg A young *parlementaire* who appeared to defend those burned for heresy, arguing that they merely stood up for the word of God. He was consequently tried and burned at the stake for heresy and treason. He had not only renounced Catholicism but also his king, arguing that no French subject had to recognise the rule of a monarch who contravened God's will. The majority of magistrates were loyal Catholics but the du Bourg incident certainly leads us to believe that other *parlementaires* were in Calvin's camp.

- The church of Paris was established in 1555 by Jean le Macon along with François de Morel and Antoine de La Roche Chandieu. The danger of detection and persecution was real, as was shown in September 1557 when an angry mob **attacked a Calvinist congregation** in the rue Saint Jacques. The congregation reflected the wide social spectrum which was attracted to the reformed faith as nobles worshipped alongside artisans.
- Despite such setbacks, the reformed movement continued to survive and expand at a **local level**. In 1558, Calvinists staged a mass demonstration in Paris when over 4,000 gathered to sing psalms on the left bank of the Seine, in clear defiance of the *parlement*.
- In 1559, French Calvinists held their first National Synod in Paris under the leadership of Morel. Pastors from ten other French Calvinist churches attended to discuss matters of organisation and doctrine. The outcome was a Confession of Faith and Ecclesiastical Discipline which were both closely modelled on Calvin's own works. For the first time Calvinism in France was organised and unified, something which was crucial if the movement was going to survive and prosper.
- A minority of Calvinist supporters in the *parlements* of Paris also helped to delay legislation unfavourable to Calvinism. Most notably **Anne du Bourg** had clear Protestant sympathies and, after personally insulting Henry II in 1559, was imprisoned along with six of his supporters and ordered to reject his religion.
- Calvinist doctrine also gave encouragement and determination to those under threat of persecution. Calvinist theories of divine providence and predestination offered the converted self-belief that they were God's elect and that ultimately they would triumph over the forces of Catholicism.

CONCLUSION: HOW SUCCESSFUL WAS CALVINISM?

- Even at its peak, between 1555 and 1562, perhaps only 10 per cent of the population were Calvinist, which equates to 1.8 million people: a large number certainly, but still a minority. 1,200 churches distributed throughout the kingdom was a major success in the face of such harsh repression, but many relied upon the protection and patronage of the nobility.

- In north-east France, where the Guises held much property, Calvinism made little headway and no missionaries ventured into Picardy, Flanders or Burgundy. Calvinism was never going to sweep all before it.
- To many of Calvin's adherents in France, their leader and figurehead was a rather distant figure who asked too much of their loyalty and commitment at times. For example, in his *Letter to the Nicodemites* written in 1544 Calvin urged his followers in France who still worshipped in secret while maintaining a façade of orthodoxy, to come out into the open and face persecution or flee the country. Some found this too severe, and in 1544 Antoine Fumee protested on behalf of French evangelicals stating that Calvin demanded the ultimate sacrifice. The issue of resistance to royal authority was raised by Anne du Bourg. Such action was too revolutionary for Calvin at this stage, but demonstrated the extremes to which some were taking the reformed reformed faith.

CHAPTER SUMMARY: THE THREAT FROM CALVINISM

Let us look at the key facts:

- Calvinism initially emerged (in the 1540s) as an urban movement in cities such as Rouen and Lyons. Calvinists have been identified as literate, self assertive and ambitious.
- Later on (during the 1550s) Calvinism thrived also in rural areas under noble protection.
- Calvinism crossed social boundaries. In Amiens Calvinists were drawn from the working classes, whereas in Lyons they were artisans and merchants.
- Calvin and Geneva played a crucial role in the development of Calvinism in France especially in the 1550s.
- *The Institutes* (1536) and *The Ordinances* (1541) provided the templates for a gathered church.

EXAM TIPS

Religion in this period is the most important theme that you will study as religious issues led to over thirty years of civil war in France which devastated the kingdom. It is therefore important that you have a clear idea of how Calvinism developed in France and why it was perceived by the vast majority of the population as a serious threat.

- By 1560 there were over 1,200 reformed churches and 1.8 million adherents. However, it is important to emphasise that 90 per cent of the population remained Catholic.
- Calvinist strongholds developed in the Midi, although again specific circumstances allowed for survival elsewhere.

What does this mean?

- The very existence of Calvinism undermined the Gallican principles that bound France together as a community of believers. The sacred oath of the monarch along with the entire social order was undermined by this religion.
- Calvinism was therefore seen as fractious, divisive and dangerous. Huguenots were not just heretics – they were seditious rebels.
- Popular, local violence increased where Calvinists and Catholics lived side-by-side (for example in Paris). This is especially the case as Huguenots became more assertive and confident in the 1550s.
- Calvinism showed an incredible ability to survive and develop beneath the cross (under repression).
- The key watershed mark was Catherine de Medici's Edict of January 1562 (see page 77) in which she offered toleration to the Huguenots. In the light of the above analysis it is clear why this enraged Catholics and sparked civil war.

The specification key themes across the period can be summarised as follows:

Nation state

One can see some continuity between Louis XII and Henry II over the issue of territorial boundaries. In 1559 Henry II signed a treaty (Cateau Cambresis) with Philip II of Spain which gave up French interests in Italy, but held on to the territories of Metz, Toul and Verdun on the north-eastern frontier of France. Once more then, we can see the gradual emergence of the modern, hexagon shape of France.

Relations between kings and subjects

One can see continuity in this area between Henry II and his predecessor Francis I. Henry continued to centralise government in order to increase monarchical power and enhance the effectiveness of his government over the kingdom. Henry II also continued to push the boundaries of taxation to their limits, resulting in open unrest in Bordeaux in 1548. With regards to the nobility, relations became strained on religious lines, a trend that would intensify and harden over the following twenty-five years.

Religious developments
Henry II's reign is a key turning point in religious developments. The emergence of Calvinism, backed by powerful noble support begins to divide the country. The ability of Calvinism to grow, despite royal persecution harms the crown, and Henry II leaves behind an unsolved religious problem for his son and successor, Francis II.

Social and economic developments
The reign of Henry II also marks something of a turning point in social and economic terms. The economic growth that had marked the beginning of the period halts and a recession begins. Tax increases had not kept pace with the cost of foreign war, and the crown was heavily in debt to foreign bankers. Inflation and unemployment marked the economic downturn, and standard of living dropped considerably. Population growth placed pressure on land and food supplies leading to shortages and poverty. Some of the blame for this recession should be laid at the door of the monarchy. French kings such as Francis I and Henry II did little to encourage trade and French merchants seemed more interested in buying offices than investing in mercantile activity. More importantly the damage that foreign policy did to the French economy was terrible, with war necessitating growing taxation demands. This trend would be exacerbated over the next twenty-five years as foreign war gave way to civil war.

QUESTIONS TO CONSIDER

1. How far did Henry II continue the policies of Francis I?

2. Explain the rise of Calvinism in France.

3. Why was Protestantism regarded as such a threat in France?

CHAPTER 5

The French Wars of Religion 1: 1562–70

WHAT WERE THE ISSUES THAT CAUSED AND SHAPED THE FRENCH WARS OF RELIGION?

KEY THEMES

Belief The historian Mack Holt emphasises the significance of religion in a social context rather than a doctrinal one, that is to say that France was made up of a vast community of believers each believing that they were the godly and the other community were misfits.

The French Wars of Religion began in 1562 with the massacre at Vassy; continued until the Edict of Nantes in 1598; and then erupted again briefly in the 1620s. This civil conflict was between two communities of **belief**, namely Catholics and Protestants (or Huguenots as French Calvinists were known). The French Wars of Religion served to divide the populace along confessional lines as well as politically and socially. One must not underestimate the importance of religion in the Wars of Religion. Political, social and economic issues were intertwined around the issue of religion.

Huguenots rejected transubstantiation and, similarly, Catholics objected to the singing of psalms in the vernacular, but it is the social backdrop to such doctrinal rejection which sets the scene for over 30 years of internal strife:

- Neither side could accept the presence of the other, so any compromise was going to be short-lived.
- Each side viewed the other as having broken God's will and, in particular, the Catholics viewed the Huguenots as dangerous and seditious rebels, threatening the accepted social and political order which had existed for centuries.

Bearing this in mind it is no surprise that there were specific acts of violent cleansing and purification, nor that the conflict lasted for so long. Religion was at the heart of the troubles but the premature death of Henry II in 1559 was the immediate cause of the problems.

The map shows France with regions and cities marked including Calais, Cambrai, Amiens, Péronne, Rouen, Le Havre, PICARDY, NORMANDY, Rheims, Strasbourg, Evreux, Mantes, Meaux, St Germain-en-Laye, Paris, Châlons-sur-Marne, Verneuil, Dreux, Vincennes, BRITTANY, Alençon, Étampes, CHAMPAGNE, Rennes, Le Mans, Fontainebleau, Sens, Châteaudun, Orléans, Auxerre, ANJOU, Angers, Blois, R. Loire, Tours, Saumur, Amboise, Nantes, Châtellerault, Bourges, La Charité, Dijon, Poitiers, BERRY, Nevers, BURGUNDY, POITOU, Châteauroux, La Rochelle, MARCHE, R. Charente, R. Saône, Mâcon, Geneva, Angoulême, Lyon, ANGOUMOIS, Vienne, Issoire, Bordeaux, R. Dordogne, Bergerac, Grenoble, Cahors, Mende, Valence, DAUPHINE, Nérac, Agen, Montauban, Largentiere, GUYENNE, R. Tarn, Orange, Bayonne, Toulouse, LANGUEDOC, Nîmes, Avignon, PROVENCE, BÉARN, Montpellier, Aix-en-Provence, Garonne, Carcassonne, Béziers, R. Lot.

Scale: 0 — 150 miles / 0 — 200 km. N (north arrow).

WHY WAS THE DEATH OF HENRY II IN 1559 A TURNING POINT IN THE DEVELOPMENT OF FRANCE?

The unexpected death of Henry II took place at a festival in celebration of the recently concluded peace treaty of Cateau-Cambrésis in July 1559. The King died as a consequence of head wounds received in a jousting accident. His death created a power vacuum at court which coincided with increased religious tensions (in part due to increasing Huguenot strength). Henry was succeeded on the throne by his 15-year-old son Francis II. Recently married to Mary Stuart, Queen of Scots, Francis was clearly inexperienced and vulnerable to political faction:

Protestant churches in 1562.

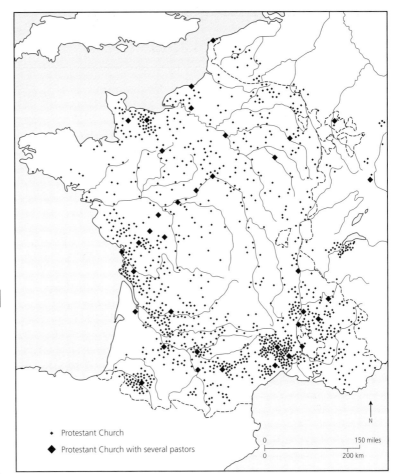

Protestant Church

Protestant Church with several pastors

0   150 miles
0   200 km

N

The Guise family Staunch Catholics, the wealthiest and principle noble family in France. As the Guise family eased into power after the death of Henry II, prospects for the Huguenots looked bleak.

Antoine de Bourbon (1518–62) Some Protestants believed that because Francis had not yet reached the age of 21 he was a minor and that the King of Navarre, namely Antoine de Bourbon, should become regent.

Catherine de Medici (1519–89) The death of Henry II in 1559 began a power struggle between his widow, Catherine de Medici, and the followers of the Duke of Guise over who should control the successive boy kings, Francis II and Charles IX. Catherine lost out over Francis but regained the regency of Charles and proceeded to pursue a policy of religious toleration towards the Huguenots.

- In particular, the **Guise** family looked to dominate court, as Mary's mother was a sister of Francis, Duke of Guise, and Charles, Cardinal of Lorraine.
- Opposed to the Guises were the mainly Huguenot Bourbon family, princes of the blood, and led by the vacillating **Antoine de Bourbon** and his more committed wife (in terms of Huguenot allegiance) Jeanne d'Albret. Louis de Bourbon, Prince of Condé and younger brother of Antoine, was also dismayed by the Guise dominance of the young King and proposed military means to counter such activity.
- The ruling house of Valois, overseen by Henry's widow, **Catherine de Medici**, objected to the domination of Francis II for other reasons. While unquestionably Catholic, Catherine wanted what was best for all four of her sons, and she was convinced that the Guise family would only look after their own interests. Catherine was a thoughtful and pragmatic lady who did not wish to see

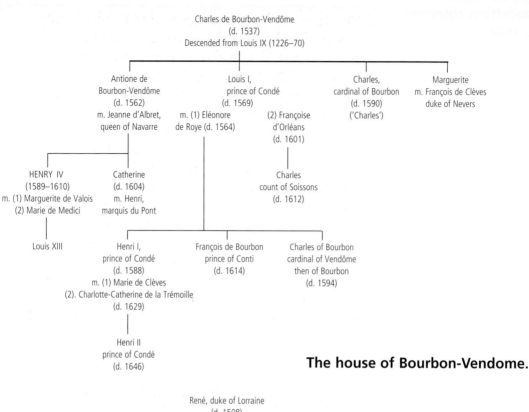

The house of Bourbon-Vendome.

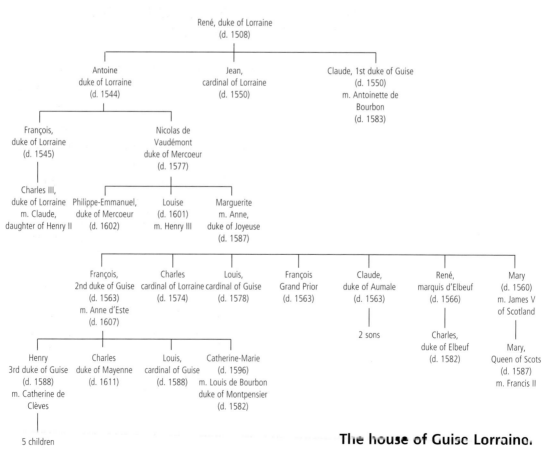

The house of Guise Lorraine.

the crown under the stranglehold of a noble family as powerful and influential as the Guises; but at first Francis himself seemed to pay more attention to his uncle, the Duke of Guise, than his mother.

- The Montmorency family was a mixture of confessional and political loyalties. Anne de Montmorency, Constable of France, was head of the family and had been a loyal and close advisor to Henry II. Steadfastly Catholic, Anne viewed heresy as a cancer which had to be taken out of French society. Yet his sister, Louise de Chatillon, favoured the Huguenots, and her three sons all became prominent members of the reformed cause. Two of Montmorency's sons Francis and Henry de Damville also joined the Huguenot movement when their own needs dictated that they do so, and when political and financial rewards were offered. Both were opportunists who looked to further their own ambitions amid monarchical weakness and religious tension.

WHAT WAS THE SIGNIFICANCE OF THE CONSPIRACY OF AMBOISE?

The drift to war began in March 1560, when a group of Huguenot nobles attempted to capture Francis II while the royal court wintered at the Château of Amboise; they wanted to liberate him from the clutches of the Guise family. The leader of the plot was Jean du Barry, Seigneur de la Renaudie. La Renaudie had consulted Louis de Bourbon and Calvin, although the latter was not willing to endorse the conspiracy. The plot was leaked to the Guises who were ready and waiting in March 1560 as the conspirators prepared to ride on the royal château. With the loss of the element of surprise, the conspirators had little chance against the royal troops under Guise's command. Several hundred Huguenots were captured and summarily hanged as traitors from the château walls. The so-called Conspiracy of Amboise had failed, but more than this it re-emphasised to Catholics all over France that the Huguenots were dangerous and seditious rebels who sought to overthrow the established order and perhaps even the crown itself.

Condé was also arrested for his links with the conspirators and would have faced execution had Francis II not died in December 1560 from an ear infection. Francis was immediately succeeded by his 9-year-old brother, Charles IX, and Guise influence at court was lost, as Catherine de Medici assumed the position of regent with Antoine de Bourbon as lieutenant-general and the overtly Protestant Gaspard de Coligny on the council. Here were the first signs of the middle course which Catherine de Medici pursued in religious policy, tolerating known Huguenots in order to create political stability. In the long term she recognised that toleration could never create stability because the bulk of the French population believed the Huguenots to be heretical rebels who undermined the monarchy and the kingdom. Nevertheless, Catherine released Condé and pursued her policy of compromise and toleration under the watchful eye of the new chancellor, Michel de l'Hopital. Both believed that a policy of toleration would restore order.

HOW SUCCESSFUL WAS CATHERINE DE MEDICI'S POLICY OF RELIGIOUS TOLERATION?

Two meetings of the Estates General in 1560 and 1561 had failed to find a solution to the religious problem, so in September 1561 Catherine took matters into her own hands and invited religious leaders from both sides to a meeting at Poissy in order to see if a middle ground could be found to reunite all Frenchmen under the Gallican church. Yet reconciliation was impossible as neither side was willing to compromise with the other:

- Theological matters of doctrine such as disagreement over the eucharist were insurmountable.
- The popular and political strength of Calvinism had perhaps hardened the Huguenots' resolve to stand their ground.

Ultra-Catholics, for their part, were entirely disillusioned with a regime which sat around the negotiating table with heretics and those such as the Guises began to make more militant noises. In late 1561, Duke Francis of Guise, Constable Montmorency and Marshal Saint André formed a military triumvirate to destroy heresy in France with Spanish aid from Philip II. France was moving closer to civil war by the day, and the threat to obliterate all Protestants merely hastened its advance.

What was the reaction to Catherine's religious policy?

In January 1562, Catherine de Medici issued the Edict of Saint Germain (the Edict of January) which proclaimed the limited but legal recognition of the Huguenots:

- Huguenots were allowed to assemble for worship outside town walls during the daytime, although they were not allowed to arm themselves, sing the psalms in public or worship freely without fear of persecution.
- Protestant nobles could organise and protect Calvinist congregations on their own estates, thus recognising the support that the reformed faith had among sections of the aristocracy.

The government had stuck to its policy of toleration in order to maintain order but, in offering legal recognition to the Huguenots, Catherine de Medici had gone too far. The edict aroused anger and resentment in the *parlement* of Paris which predictably refused to register the edict until ordered to do so by Catherine herself. A formal **remonstrance** was sent to the Queen Mother emphasising the king's duty to defend the one true faith, Catholicism, as outlined in his coronation oath, an oath which Charles was yet to take. The *parlement* finally registered the edict on 6 March 1562, but with an amendment attached stating that it was against its will and only because the king had expressly commanded that it do so. Yet by this time such objections were insignificant because the edict had already proved to be unenforceable.

On 1 March 1562, the Duke of Guise and a group of armed followers had come upon a group of Huguenots worshipping within the town walls of Vassy, in Champagne, a contravention of the January Edict. Guise and his followers killed the unarmed worshippers and marched on Paris in order to raise a Catholic army. In response to the massacre, the Protestants held a National Synod at Orleans where it was agreed that troops should be mobilised under the leadership of Louis de Bourbon, Prince of Condé. Two opposing camps, both armed, now faced each other, and France was on the brink of a civil war which would span three generations and result in political and economic ruin.

WHAT WERE THE CHARACTERISTICS OF THE FIRST THREE WARS OF RELIGION?

The first three Wars of Religion are characterised by local tension, stalemate on the battlefield and inadequate peace settlements which served to spark off further violence. As the wars progressed in this period we see the steady decline of central authority and the growing hostilities in local communities which would ultimately result in the St Bartholomew's Day Massacre of 1572.

The First War of Religion, 1563: The call to arms

The initial conflict which began in 1562 saw a number of powerful nobles take up the military leadership of the reformed cause. Condé and Coligny were the leading lights and their large clientele network throughout Picardy and Normandy respectively ensured further aristocratic support. The third National Synod met at Orleans in April 1562: Condé was proclaimed protector of all the Calvinist churches in France and of the house and crown of France. Armed resistance to the Guise family was declared, and significantly, little mention was made of pastors, ministers or even Geneva. The fate of Protestantism in France appeared to be in the hands of the rural nobility.

Catherine de Medici was helpless in the face of military mobilisation on both sides, and she could only watch as Guise was given a hero's welcome into Paris after Vassy.

- The Catholic military **triumvirate** which had orchestrated the massacre was able to recruit Antoine de Bourbon, King of Navarre, who gave up his mild Protestant sympathies and threw in his lot with the Guise faction.

KEY TERMS

Triumvirate A military alliance of three key noblemen.

- From his base in Orleans, Condé directed operations, and the Huguenots built fortified strongholds throughout Guyenne, Languedoc and Dauphine either through military conquest or genuine conversion of the municipal magistrates. With Orleans, Rouen, Lyons and Tours in Huguenot hands in 1563 control of the major waterways and land routes became a priority. The Queen Mother now had little option but to back the triumvirate and endorse religious war.
- Guise dispatched Catholic forces to lay siege to Huguenot towns in the north in an attempt to split Condé's forces in two and disrupt communications. Eventually, towns such as Rouen, Blois and Tours were won back by Guise but at a cost. Antoine de Bourbon was fatally wounded during the siege of Rouen while the three months it had taken for that city to submit, demonstrated to the triumvirate how difficult it would be to overturn all of the fortified strongholds which the Huguenots possessed.
- In December 1562, the only major engagement of the first war was fought at Dreux, and although the Catholics were victorious, Marshal Saint André was killed while rival commanders Condé and Montmorency were captured. Worse was to follow for the Catholics as

The three Guise brothers, leaders of the Catholic cause: left to right, Cardinal of Lorraine, Henry of Lorraine and Duke of Mayenne.

Duke Francis of Guise was assassinated while besieging Orleans in February 1563. Two of the original triumvirate were dead and the other was being held captive. Stalemate now ensued on the battlefield.

- Outright victory for the Catholics was impossible and Catherine de Medici took this opportunity to draw up a peace settlement. Having secured the release of Montmorency and Condé, the peace process began and resulted in the **Edict of Amboise** (March 1563).

What was the significance of the First War of Religion?

The first war set a trend which was followed until 1598 and the Edict of Nantes. Neither side was capable of gaining outright victory over the other and, with resources expended, a compromise peace settlement was concluded which was unenforceable and entirely inadequate. It was only a matter of time before the conflict was resumed, and both sides knew it. The personnel might be slightly different, especially on the Catholic side, but the roots of the problem and the nature of the conflict remained the same.

Why did the peace not hold?

Once again the *parlement* of Paris led the way in refusing to ratify the Edict of Amboise because it offered legal recognition to Calvinism. Registration was provisional upon the king reaching his age of majority; attached to the ratification was an explicit remonstrance. In reply, Catherine took a swipe at the perceived arrogance of the *parlement* of Paris by proclaiming the majority of Charles IX in the *parlement* of Rouen. The declaration was in the form of a *lit de justice*, a rare event which typified Catherine's desire to re-impose order through the crown. Between 1564 and 1566 Charles IX and his mother along with the chancellor l'Hopital and the rest of the household undertook a royal progress through the provinces to display the King in his year of majority to his subjects, as well as ensure that all the *parlement*s ratified the peace edict. Catherine also hoped for the support of moderate nobles who shared her vision of peace through toleration. Yet while acknowledged as a success, the progress also demonstrated to Catherine how unpopular her edict was and how unenforceable it was in practice. Local tensions were made worse by the clauses offering toleration; in particular, Catholic violence towards Huguenots became more common.

How did the Second War of Religion begin?

At court the dominant faction was still the Guise family despite the assassination of Duke Francis. The deceased Duke's two brothers, Claude, Duke of Aumale, and Charles, Cardinal of Lorraine, continued to press for a resumption of hostilities; the family issued a vendetta against Admiral Coligny whom they suspected of organising the assassination of Francis. Worryingly for Catherine, Henry, Duke of Anjou, younger brother of Charles IX and heir to the throne, was heavily influenced by Charles, Cardinal of Lorraine, while Condé and Coligny had stopped attending council meetings altogether. Once again, Catherine's vision of peace was slowly disintegrating and a second war that lasted almost six months broke out in September 1567.

The war began over Huguenot fears that a Spanish army marching along France's eastern frontier to get to the **Netherlands** was going to change course and confront the Huguenots on the battlefield. Such suspicions were not unreasonable given the political circumstances. The Catholics had received aid from Philip II in the form of troops to fight in Guyenne during the first war. Also, in June 1565, Catherine herself had met with her daughter, the Queen of Spain, and the **Duke of Alva** at Bayonne, and there is little doubt that Alva attempted to persuade her to take a more aggressive and hard line towards the Protestants in France. The same Alva led the Spanish troops across eastern France in 1567.

Although we now know that Catherine had no intention of attacking the Protestant leadership in 1567, the rumours and fears were enough to prompt Coligny and Condé to organise another plot to kidnap the King and free him from the clutches of the Guise faction. The coup was nearly a success as Huguenot forces mobilised rapidly and a number of local risings took Catholic leaders by surprise. However, the main event, like the previous attempt at

KEY EVENTS

Situation in the Netherlands A number of Protestant riots had broken out in the Spanish-controlled southern Netherlands in the summer of 1566. The rioters smashed religious images. They were loosely inspired by Calvinism although Calvin himself was critical of such destruction. The advance of Calvinism in the Netherlands and the Dutch struggle for independence from Habsburg/Spanish oppression were interlinked.

KEY PEOPLE

Duke of Alva (1508–82) Alva was a Spanish general who arrived in the Netherlands in 1567 to enforce Spanish control. After establishing the Council of Blood which ruthlessly persecuted those involved in the revolt of 1566, Alva proceeded to defeat William of Orange, entering Brussels in triumph in 1568. Recalled to Spain in 1573, he later commanded a successful invasion of Portugal in 1581.

Amboise in 1560, was not a success, and war effectively broke out when the royal court at Meaux heard that Condé's troops had mobilised in September 1567. In 1568 the second war ended with the **Edict of Longjumeau**.

Hostility to the peace was greatest in Paris and right from the start the Cardinal of Lorraine worked to overturn the peace settlement. The Cardinal outlined a plot to seize a number of Huguenot towns such as Orleans and La Rochelle and in the process capture Condé and Coligny. The plot was forced through the royal council in August 1568, an indication of how the Guise faction now dominated affairs. Moderates like l'Hopital were sidelined and the Queen Mother along with Charles IX himself were little more than bystanders. Henry, Duke of Anjou, on the other hand had been appointed lieutenant-general of the army, effectively taking on the role left vacant by Montmorency. The loyalties of Anjou were clear, and his own political advancement rode on the back of his affiliation to the Cardinal of Lorraine rather than his mother. The plot to strike at the heart of Huguenot power predictably failed, and the Protestant leaders fled to La Rochelle.

The Third War, 1568–70: Why did this war of religion last longer than the previous two?

The peace of Longjumeau proved to be the most short-lived of the Wars of Religion, and the Third War was the most destructive, thus demonstrating the rise in tension and hostility between the faiths and the increasing strength and organisation of both sides on the battlefield. The Third War was also longer than the previous two, probably as a consequence of increased foreign support for the Huguenots:

- In August 1568, Condé and Coligny signed a formal treaty of mutual support with the Dutch nobleman in exile **William of Orange**. Both had a common enemy in Philip II – Orange had narrowly escaped execution in June 1568 after a failed revolt against Spanish power in the Netherlands while the Spanish King had encouraged the Cardinal of Lorraine to violate the peace of Longjumeau and renew hostilities. Orange could not

Edict of Longjumeau (March 1568) Allowed for the legal worship of Calvinism in the suburbs of one town in each *bailliage*, as well as on noble estates.

KEY PEOPLE

William of Orange (1533–84) The father of Dutch independence and hero of the Dutch struggle against the Catholic Spanish. A failure in 1566 and again in 1568, Orange led a more successful revolt in 1572 leading to the Pacification of Ghent in which all seventeen Dutch provinces were united against Spain. However, the alliance was short-lived as the southern provinces returned to the Spanish fold. William continued to campaign for religious toleration and conciliation. He courted the French Duke of Anjou as a sovereign figurehead for the northern provinces in revolt with limited success. In 1584, Orange was assassinated leaving the United Provinces of the north leaderless.

Mary, Queen of Scots (niece of the Cardinal of Lorraine), had been forced to flee Scotland in 1568 as a consequence of a Calvinist, noble revolution and she threw herself upon the mercy of Elizabeth. Mary was next in line to the English throne as long as Elizabeth remained childless. For this reason Elizabeth had her imprisoned, fearful of the scheming of Lorraine. Lorraine's plan was to marry off Anjou to Mary and unite the two crowns under Catholicism. Such thoughts naturally pushed Elizabeth closer to Condé and Coligny.

offer the Huguenots a great deal of aid given his own precarious situation in 1568 but the German states and England were a different story.

- Wolfgang Wilhelm of Zweibrucken offered 8,000 reiters and 40 ensigns of foot which were paid for by Elizabeth I. **Ties between the Huguenots and the English Queen** were growing ever stronger.

What was the significance of the Peace of St Germain in 1570?

The peace edict which ended the Third War of Religion reflected Huguenot strength on the battlefield and their victory at Arnay-le-Duc, and the terms were the most favourable yet to the Huguenots. With the Cardinal of Lorraine disgraced and out of favour, the council agreed on more specific terms:

- Protestant worship was permitted inside two towns per government region and the towns were actually specified to avoid dispute or ambiguity.
- The Protestants were also allowed to occupy four fortified towns for a two-year period, namely La Rochelle, Cognac, Montauban and La Charité.
- Provisions were also made to reintegrate Huguenots into French society such as equality in taxation and the right to hold offices. All property seized from Huguenots from 1562 onwards was to be returned. On the whole, the edict reflected major royal concessions of toleration. Not only could Protestants worship freely inside the walls of certain towns for the first time, but they were able to consolidate their military position in the south-west through the creation of fortified towns. After three civil wars and eight years of bloodshed, the Catholic forces seemed no nearer to eliminating heresy.

CHAPTER SUMMARY: THE FIRST THREE WARS OF RELIGION

There are many key themes which emerge during these first three Wars of Religion:

- The pattern of military stalemate, unenforceable peace edicts and renewed conflict created a vicious circle of civil violence which continued until 1598.
- **Foreign aid** for both Huguenots and Catholics was crucial in supplementing the respective armies.
- Catherine de Medici, Charles IX and Chancellor l'Hopital pursued a middle course to restore peace and order through toleration. Yet in undermining the Gallican principles which bound French society together they misjudged the intensity of belief within French society. Catholics in particular could not tolerate living alongside 'seditious heretics' and events such as the conspiracy of Amboise reinforced their view of Protestants as traitors. Any peace settlement that offered toleration to the Huguenots was unlikely to last for any length of time.
- Outright military victory on the battlefield was unachievable for either side during this period although one might have expected the royal army to triumph given its superior resources and personnel. Indeed Anjou had his chance after Montcour in 1569 but chose instead to lay siege to St Jean d'Angely. In general however such opportunities were few and far between.
- The royal forces found it difficult to mobilise quickly, and to get troops into the south west in order to launch an effective strike. Foreign mercenaries made up the bulk of the royal army and they were costly and had to be recruited from abroad. Also, if they were not paid regularly they became disgruntled and dissatisfied. Huguenot strongholds were difficult to breach and they were well dispersed throughout the kingdom. The royal forces were not able to target one particular town, and sieges were costly both in terms of money and lives. During the 1560s the crown spent an average 4.6 million livres per annum to maintain its army in the field. The war was taking up nearly half of the royal revenue and was rapidly sapping royal finances.
- The Huguenots were in a minority (only ten per cent of the population) but they were well organised, disciplined and committed. The religious environment elsewhere in Europe, such as in the Netherlands or in the Palatinate, ensured foreign aid, while the hierarchical structure of the Calvinist Church in France allowed funds to be

EXAM TIPS

You will not be expected to recount the details of individual battles in the examination but it is important that you understand the key themes that we can see emerging over the first three religious wars.

KEY THEMES

Foreign Aid Both sides relied heavily on Swiss and German mercenaries, but the Huguenots desperately needed the financial and logistical support given to them by Elector Frederick III, the Duke of Zweibrucken, Elizabeth I and William of Orange. Foreign support served to internationalise the conflict and prolong the wars.

raised with relative ease. Strong fortified towns along the Loire and in the south-west were easy to defend and did not put vast numbers of lives at risk.

- Condé and Coligny managed their armies and resources more effectively than Anjou or even Tavennes. The Huguenot leaders avoided pitched battles wherever possible and settled for a more defensive strategy until Coligny was able to take advantage of a weak royal force in 1570, and thus put the Huguenots in a relatively strong position.

The specification key themes across the period can be summarised as follows:

Nation state

Civil conflict damages any sort of move towards a nation state. One can hardly talk of national unity when Frenchmen were at war with themselves. All aspects of religious, political and social unity were challenged by the emergence of Calvinism and the onset of civil war. In this light, religion is the main challenge to the emergence of a nation state in France in the sixteenth century.

Relations between kings and subjects

The premature death of Henry II weakens the monarchy at a crucial time and opens up the court to factional conflict. The power of the crown weakens under a female regent and the power of certain noble groups increases. At a provincial level, civil war weakens monarchical authority in the localities and much of the work done by Francis I and Henry II to centralise government is shown up to be rather superficial during this period of civil war.

Religious developments

Calvinism fuelled the civil conflict and although there were clearly political dimensions and implications to the fighting, it was religion that was at the heart of the troubles. French society was divided along religious lines, and it appeared almost inevitable that there would be an outpouring of popular religious violence in those areas where a sizeable Protestant minority existed alongside a Catholic majority. On the political side, noble support for Calvinism remained the key to its survival.

Social and economic developments

There would have been an economic downturn in France, with or without civil war, but the internal conflict served to exacerbate the recession. Civil war severely damaged French agriculture, trade and commerce. Exports of wine from Brittany and textile manufacturing in Amiens were crippled by the conflict whilst consistent defaulting on foreign loans by the crown ruined Lyon as a financial centre. Rising taxes in the localities placed unbearable pressures on the third estate, and popular risings became more frequent. Local tax collectors were even more ruthless than those previously employed by the crown, and soon the peasantry were heavily in debt or had vacated their farms.

QUESTIONS TO CONSIDER

1. Why did Catherine de Medici's policies of conciliation at Poissy fail?

2. Who supported Calvinism in French society?

3. Why did civil war break out in 1562?

4. Why were the royal forces unable to defeat the Huguenots in the first eight years of the conflict?

CHAPTER 6

The French Wars of Religion 2: St Bartholomew's Day, 1572

WHAT WERE THE CAUSES OF THE ST BARTHOLOMEW'S DAY MASSACRE?

Historical controversy surrounds the St Bartholomew's Day Massacre and our understanding of the events is not helped by the unreliability of most of the contemporary material. Two sequences of events are crucial which together make up the massacre.

- The first is the attempted assassination of Coligny that took place on 22 August 1572, along with the murder of several dozen Huguenot leaders, on the morning of 24 August.
- The second sequence is inextricably linked to the first: the popular wave of killings which broke out in Paris between 24 and 27 August and which were mimicked across the provinces throughout September and October.

The situation in France following the Edict of Saint Germain was more favourable to the Protestants than at any previous time, and prospects for a lasting peace appeared to be good. Provisions had been made for the reintegration of Huguenots into French society and Catherine de Medici was arranging two marriage alliances to strengthen her peace policy:

- The first was between Henry, Duke of Anjou, and Queen Elizabeth of England. It fell through when Anjou came under predictable pressure from the Guise faction to denounce the heretical Queen of England. Catherine then put forward her youngest son, Francis, Duke of Alençon, as a potential suitor for Elizabeth but with similar results.
- The second marriage was probably more contentious but easier to arrange. Catherine wanted to marry her daughter, Marguerite, to the Protestant King of Navarre. In the eyes of the Queen Mother this Huguenot–

Catholic matrimonial bond would be symbolic of the new era of the peace of Saint Germain.

What evidence is there that religious tensions were increasing?

The numbers of conversions to Protestantism were beginning to fall and had reached their pinnacle in the late 1560s. But there were serious outbreaks of violence on both sides:

- Protestant attitudes were becoming more extreme and several Protestant texts **attacked the Gallican monarchy** and the authority of the king. These texts served to polarise attitudes and horrified Catholics who held the monarchy to be at the core of French society.
- Moreover, religious tensions among the community at large were on the increase after Saint Germain. Catholic mob violence in Paris and in the provinces became more common. In November 1571, the removal of the **Croix de Gastines** to another location under a clause in the Edict of Saint Germain, sparked off rioting which led to over 40 deaths. In Rouen, armed Catholics massacred

Attack on the Gallican monarchy *The Declaration and Protestation of those of the Reformed Religion in La Rochelle* went so far as to suggest that kings had no right to command the consciences of their subjects. Kings such as Charles IX could rule by God's will, only if they followed God's will, and such pamphlets advocated popular sovereignty.

Croix de Gastines This large cross was erected in Paris in 1569 to symbolise the just execution of two Huguenots. The Peace of Saint Germain (1570) specified that all such monuments to the persecution of Huguenots be torn down. The order provoked riots among the Catholic Parisian mob.

Protestant strongholds, 1562.

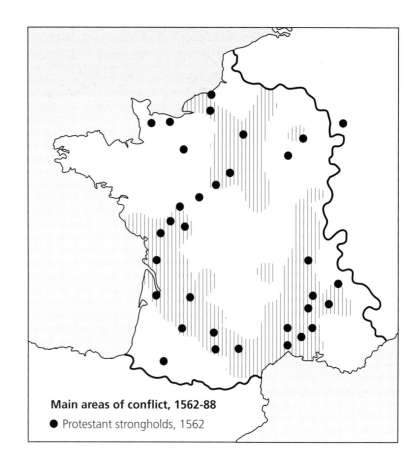

Main areas of conflict, 1562-88
● Protestant strongholds, 1562

another 40 Huguenots after an earlier altercation over the Corpus Christi.

Religious tensions were ready to boil over at a popular level and communities, especially Catholic ones, were willing and ready to take matters into their own hands in order to preserve the 'one true faith'.

KEY EVENTS

Renewed war against the Habsburgs After the Sea Beggars captured Brill in April 1572, sparking off the Revolt of the Netherlands, there is evidence to suggest that Charles IX, under the influence of Coligny, was ready to enter a war against Spain on the side of the Dutch rebels.

WHY WAS THERE AN ATTEMPT TO ASSASSINATE COLIGNY IN 1572?

Between 1570 and 1572 Coligny's power on the royal council increased, at the expense of the Guise family. Coligny was eager to persuade Catherine that a renewed **war against the Habsburgs** over the Netherlands might reunite the country. Yet Coligny was in a minority on the royal council in wanting war and even he could not promise to control the French Huguenots who wanted to join the fight in the Netherlands against Philip II. Charles was rapidly going off the idea of war by August 1572 although Coligny's warmongering policy should not be seen as a reason for Catherine wanting him dead. Indeed, if her marriage alliance between Marguerite and Navarre was to be a success, she would require Coligny's support. Therefore, it appears difficult to argue that Catherine was the driving force behind the plot to assassinate Coligny. Yet, it was the royal wedding, orchestrated by Catherine, on 18 August 1572 which provided the backdrop for the St Bartholomew's Day Massacre.

The series of killings collectively known as the St Bartholomew's Day Massacre began on 22 August 1572 with the attempted assassination of Gaspard de Coligny. The admiral had remained in Paris with several other Huguenot leaders after the royal wedding in order to discuss recent violations of the edict of Saint Germain with Charles IX. While returning from a meeting with the King in the Louvre, Coligny was shot in the arm and hand. The attempt to assassinate Coligny failed, and the wounded admiral along with the other Huguenot leaders took the decision to remain in Paris. Had **Sieur de Maurevert** been successful in killing Coligny it is likely that the other leaders would have fled the capital and simply regrouped and prepared for a fourth war. As it was, their fateful decision to stay allowed the ensuing massacre to take place. Charles IX promised to apprehend the assassin, but most Huguenots were talking of revenge rather than justice. As for who arranged the assassination, it is unlikely to have been the work of Catherine and more likely to have been arranged by the Guises.

HOW DID THE FAILED ASSASSINATION ATTEMPT LEAD TO A MASSACRE?

The assassination attempt on Coligny's life was an attempt to kill the Huguenot leader, rather than the first part of a plan to massacre all Huguenots in Paris. Yet a massacre did occur and just how this came to be and who was responsible are still shrouded in mystery:

- A royal council meeting was held on 23 August to discuss the attempt on Coligny's life and the increasing tensions within the capital. Fears abounded of a Protestant revenge attack and Catherine was panicked into making the decision to remove the Huguenot leaders.
- Rumours were circulating of 4,000 Huguenot troops commanded by Coligny's brother-in-law Teligny who were stationed just outside Paris. Many Catholics believed that the Huguenots were ready to strike against the Guises and all other Catholics in Paris. Charles was persuaded to authorise the murder of key Huguenot leaders including Coligny.
- A decision was therefore taken at the council meeting to carry out a strike against the Huguenot leaders.

Between three and four in the morning of Sunday 24 August 1572, 100 Swiss guards led by Duke Henry of Guise carried out a series of murders with Coligny being one of the first victims. The admiral was slain by Guise himself and then his body was thrown out of the window onto the street below. The **murder of Coligny** was followed by several dozen others, but the killing did not stop there.

WHAT HAPPENED BETWEEN 24 AND 27 AUGUST 1572?

The general massacre of Huguenots began on Sunday 24 August and lasted for three days. Fanatical Catholics among the city militia led the way but ordinary Parisians driven to a collective zeal joined in the carnage. Among the first non-noble victims of the general massacre were wealthy Huguenot merchants, perhaps suggesting long-term popular resentment and jealousy. Other victims included Nicolas Le Mercier who had been attacked before during the Gastines affair. The manner in which the Huguenots were murdered tells us much about Catholic hatred towards Protestantism:

- The youngest daughter of Nicolas Le Mercier was dipped naked in the blood of her massacred father and mother

KEY EVENTS

Coligny's murder Coligny was murdered at 4 am on 24 August 1572 in the Hotel de Bethisy by members of the king's guard led by Guise. His body was thrown out of the window. Coligny's head was then hacked off and taken to the royal palace in order that the Queen Mother and Charles could be satisfied that the deed was done. A mob which had gathered outside the Hotel de Bethisy further mutilated the headless corpse and dragged it through the city for three days before it was hung up at the gibbet of Mautfaucon.

The massacre of St Bartholomew's Day.

KEY FILM

Watch *La Reine Margot* **(1994)** starring Isabelle Adjani and Daniel Autevil. Based on the novel by Alexandre Dumas, this film offers a shining visual re-enactment of St Bartholomew's Day.

and baptised with threats that she would follow her family into hell if she ever became a Huguenot.

- Antoine Mulenchon, with a sword held to his throat, was told to invoke the Virgin Mary and the saints and renounce Calvinism. He refused to be reconverted and was slaughtered.
- The corpse of the wife of Mathurin Lussault was turned on a spit like a wild boar before being dragged through the streets of Paris and dumped in the Seine.

By Wednesday 27 August over 2,000 Huguenots had been murdered in Paris.

WHAT WAS THE ROLE OF CHARLES IX IN THE MASSACRE?

In seeking to explain such bloodshed we must understand that many Catholic citizens believed they were acting with **royal approval**. Ultimately, Charles would take responsibility for the massacre although he did state that the crown was faced with a Protestant coup on Saturday night and was forced to act. One immediate consequence of the King's admission of guilt was that he gained credibility among the ultra-Catholics within Paris, and attention was momentarily taken away from Henry, Duke of Guise. In reality, the King probably agreed to a plot to murder the Huguenot leaders, but Guise's words were overheard by Catholic militants and the royal authorisation

KEY THEMES

Royal approval In her work *Beneath the Cross*, (1993) Barbara Diefendorf argues that the link between the initial murders and the general massacre were the words of Guise during the murder of Coligny. Guise supposedly cried 'It is the king's command', a royal endorsement for murder which was probably taken out of context by Parisians in the neighbourhood of the Hotel de Bethisy but which spread rapidly. Diefendorf says *'these words transformed private passion into public duty'*. Certainly the evidence suggests that Parisians believed the massacre to be lawful and just; a recognition that the King had finally come to his senses.

God's will In her work, *The Rites of Violence*, Natalie Zemon Davis successfully argues that the murders carried out on St Bartholomew's Day were not random or irrational but were deliberately and purposefully carried out. Huguenots were symbolically dehumanised in ritual killings that symbolised the heretical and seditious nature of their beliefs.

Catholic compassion Philip Duplessis Mornay was sheltered by the host of the Golden Compass. Even Duke Henry of Guise harboured a young Protestant girl and attempted to prevent unnecessary slaughter. Therefore, the idea of frenzied Catholic slaughter is not entirely true.

for massacre spread rapidly throughout the city. There is even evidence to suggest that Charles tried to halt the general massacre once it broke out. Some Catholics in Paris on St Bartholomew's Day believed that they were carrying out **God's will** in the slaughter of Huguenots. Catholic preachers and literature had become more violent after the Edict of Saint Germain in the belief that God was becoming angry with the citizens of Paris for living alongside heretics. Parisians feared God's wrath for their sins and this community of believers acted on divine authority as they set about purifying the city of heretics.

Nevertheless, only a minority of Parisians took part in the violence, although the majority approved of the cleansing. There was **Catholic compassion** towards Huguenot neighbours. Protestant propaganda which laid the blame for the general massacre upon Guise, Anjou and the Queen Mother is therefore suspect. Certainly the court ought to have foreseen the violence which would follow Coligny's murder and the court might have prevented the massacre, but there is nothing to suggest that they specifically planned or ordered it.

HOW DID THE VIOLENCE SPREAD TO THE PROVINCES?

The violence in Paris spread to the provinces, specifically the urban centres of Bordeaux, Lyons, Orleans, Rouen and Toulouse:

- These were towns which were controlled by Catholics but which contained a significant Protestant minority.
- Some of these towns, such as Rouen and Orleans, had even been taken over during the first three conflicts by a Huguenot minority, so feelings and tension ran high.
- Solely Huguenot or Catholic strongholds did not witness violence in the wake of the Parisian slaughter; instead it was those towns with sizeable Huguenot minorities that saw bloodshed.

Over 3,000 Huguenots were killed in the provinces by Catholics encouraged by the events in Paris, and equally certain that they were carrying out the will of God and King.

The consequences of St Bartholomew's Day 1572

- More than 5,000 Huguenots were killed. Previous confessional violence and tension built up fervour which overspilled on St Bartholomew's Day, 1572. The massacre in Paris and subsequently in the provinces was the most dramatic and extensive in a line of confessional hatred and violence.
- The Huguenot leadership was devastated by the massacre, and with Coligny dead most Calvinists looked to **Henry of Navarre** as their figurehead. Thousands of Huguenots reconverted to Catholicism after the massacre.
- The majority of Huguenots were disillusioned with their religion and believed that God had deserted them and that Catholicism was the one true faith after all. Others abandoned Calvinism to preserve their lives. Over 3,000 Huguenots in Rouen became Catholics. Many left France altogether and went into exile in Geneva and London. Numerically Calvinism would never recover from the St Bartholomew's Day Massacre and those who remained felt isolated and vulnerable.
- The most immediate consequence of the massacres was the resumption of war. The Fourth War of Religion began in November 1572 after the Huguenot stronghold of La Rochelle refused to admit the royal governor or pay allegiance to the king.

WAR CONTINUES

What happened in the Fourth War of Religion?

Although many Catholics hoped that the St Bartholomew's Day Massacre and its aftermath would signal an end to Protestantism in France, they were wrong. Huguenot strongholds across the south-west ensured not only the survival of their faith, but also the continuation of the wars. La Rochelle on the west coast of Poitou became the centre of the Fourth War after its Huguenot magistrates refused to admit entry to the Catholic royal governor Armand de Gontaut, Marshall Biron.

On 6 November 1572, Charles IX declared war on La Rochelle, determined to make the city submit to the royal will. Hampered by logistical problems, the siege of La Rochelle directed by Biron did not begin until February 1573. The siege appeared doomed through a combination of factors:

KEY PEOPLE

Henry of Anjou (1551–89) and Francis of Alençon (1555–84)
Alençon was jealous of his elder brother's status and military record, while it was also suggested that members of Alençon's entourage were in league with the Huguenots and were conspiring to stage a coup headed by the Count of Montgomery, who was at this time still in exile in England.

KEY EVENTS

Death of Sigismund
Augustus Sigismund died leaving no male heirs. Catherine de Medici was determined to secure the Polish throne for her son Henry of Anjou. On 29 May 1573, Henry learned of his election to the Polish throne.

The Peace of La Rochelle, 1573 When contrasted with that of Saint Germain in 1570, La Rochelle effectively demonstrates the extent to which the Huguenot position had changed in those three years, primarily as a consequence of the massacres.

- Huguenot resistance was firm. The commitment of the population of La Rochelle should not be underestimated in repelling Biron's forces. The town withstood the siege for five months, bolstered by the arrival of refugees in exile after the horrific events of 1572.
- Rumours of discontent and treason abounded among the Catholic forces especially between the King's two brothers, **Henry of Anjou and Francis of Alençon**.
- The location of La Rochelle on the Atlantic coast also made it easy for supplies to be shipped in to the city, and close relations had built up between the Huguenot fortress and Protestant governments in England and the Netherlands.

In the end the peace settlement came about in May 1573 as a consequence of the **death of Sigismund Augustus**, King of Poland and Henry of Anjou's election as his successor. One of the regulations drawn up by the leader of the Polish Church called for freedom of worship in Poland and Henry felt that a show of good will in France would do no harm.

The siege at La Rochelle was draining royal finances, as it was costing over 500,000 livres per month. There were over 12,000 royal casualties and munition stocks were depleted. Peace was a necessity for the crown.

WHAT WAS THE SIGNIFICANCE OF THE PEACE OF LA ROCHELLE?

On 2 July 1573, the **peace of La Rochelle** was signed allowing Huguenot worship in the private homes of La

Rochelle, Montauban and Nîmes. Everywhere else in the kingdom, Protestant worship was banned outright. Yet the Huguenots had not been exterminated, and throughout the Midi, royal ordinances were being ignored including the latest peace settlement. Catholic suspicions increased after the Huguenots attempted to free the still captive Navarre along with Alençon in the spring of 1574. Shortly afterwards in May 1574, Charles IX died and was succeeded by his brother Henry of Anjou, King of Poland. Henry returned from Cracow to rule over a kingdom which was becoming increasingly polarised along confessional lines.

Huguenot resistance

Deprived of leadership after 1572, Huguenot policy became increasingly directed by local leaders in the south. Huguenot leaders of the reformed faith assembled in late 1572 in Languedoc to draw up a defensive alliance and, more significantly, the **Huguenot constitution** of an independent state.

In some respects a state within a state had been formed although it should be noted that the delegates at the meeting at Millau in 1574 denied that they wanted to remove the king as their lord and protector:

- The constitution was inherently anti-monarchical because it was now the federal assemblies who appointed the protector rather than the king.
- Taxes would be set and raised locally and powers of legislation were similarly self-governed.

By 1574, the Huguenot leaders from the Midi had also allied themselves to the governor of Languedoc, **Henry of Damville**, son of Anne de Montmorency. Disillusioned with royal policy he became protector of the Huguenot constitution, thus emphasising the depths of division that existed within French society.

What do Huguenot resistance theories tell us about the impact of St Bartholomew's Day?

Other more radical **resistance theories** began to emerge in the wake of the St Bartholomew's Day Massacre:

Resistance theories are useful
evidence in writing an essay on
monarchical power. Clearly the
advance of Protestantism
undermines monarchical power
in many ways. Such resistance
theories underscore the point
that the St Bartholomew's Day
Massacre changed the nature of
the conflict and in particular
moved **Huguenot attitudes** to
a more radical position.

KEY CONCEPTS

Huguenot attitudes The
concept of a United Provinces
in the Midi combined with a
call to arms against the Valois
dynasty were a severe attack on
Gallican values, and represented
a more radical stance.
Huguenot strength may have
been severely curtailed by the
massacres but the movement
was also radicalised by the
carnage.

- In *Francogallia* (1573) Francis Hotman argued that the French monarchy was elective not hereditary. Theodore de Beza took Hotman's views one step further with his *Du Droit des Magistrats* (1574) which took the line that not only were subjects not required to obey a tyrannical king but also that it was the duty of the magistrates to overthrow such a monarch. Both authors called upon the Estates General to resist the French king and represent the rights of the people.
- More influential was the *French Alarm Bell* (1574) by Nicolas Barnaud which attacked the crown over its authorisation of the St Bartholomew's Day Massacre. It urged princes and peers to overthrow tyrannical monarchs, and included a draft of the Huguenot constitution endorsing popular sovereignty.
- The *Defence of Liberty against Tyrants* (1579), written by Philippe Duplessis Mornay, argued that it was lawful to resist a tyrannical monarch.

What was the Catholic response?

In response to such revolutionary literature came Jean Bodin's principles of absolute sovereignty. In *The Six Books of the Commonwealth* (1576) Bodin stated that:

- all political authority came from God and therefore kings were answerable to God alone
- the king was an instrument of God's will
- in order for a government to be efficient the king required a council of advisers, to make laws to provide a link between master and subjects
- although the king was not a law unto himself he could not be deposed by his subjects.

Thus Bodin, a political theorist from Angers, led the way in defending the sacred nature of the monarchy.

CHAPTER SUMMARY

The specification key themes across the period can be summarised as follows:

Nation state

The St Bartholomew's Day Massacre can be used as an example of the extent to which French society had been divided along religious lines. The massacre demonstrates the importance of Catholicism to the unity of France at a social level, and without this unity the emergence of a nation state would seem some way off.

Relations between kings and subjects

The emergence of Huguenot resistance theories in the wake of St Bartholomew's Day shows us how detached a minority of the population have become from Gallican principles and the idea of a monarch appointed by God to rule over his subjects. Relations between the king and his Huguenot subjects have clearly broken down as they no longer view him as their rightful king. In the longer term, Catholics will also challenge the Valois right to rule on the grounds that they have been unable to remove the Protestant threat from France.

Religious developments

St Bartholomew's Day is a key example to highlight how important religion was at a social level. Parisian Catholics wanted to believe that the massacre was God's will as well as that of the King himself. The ritualistic way in which Huguenots were killed highlights the significance of religious loyalties to ordinary people.

Social and economic developments

A German sociologist, Max Weber argued that Calvinists worked harder than Catholics and were more disciplined and devoted to the pursuit of profit. The St Bartholomew's Day Massacre and subsequent triumph of Catholicism is in his eyes one of the main reasons why the French economy suffered in the late sixteenth and early seventeenth centuries. Whilst his research and ideas have been challenged by other academics in recent years as being flawed and too generalised, it is true that the French economy failed to keep pace with its two (Protestant) rivals in the early modern period, namely England and the Netherlands.

QUESTIONS TO CONSIDER

1. Who was to blame for the St Bartholomew's Day Massacre?

2. What does the way in which Huguenots were killed on St Bartholomew's Day reveal about popular Catholic attitudes towards Huguenots?

3. How did St Bartholomew's Day change the nature of the Protestant movement in France?

4. What was the significance of resistance theories?

CHAPTER 7

The French Wars of Religion 3: The reign of Henry III, 1574–89

ACCESSION OF HENRY III

What was the character of Henry III?

Henry of Anjou, an experienced military campaigner, but with little political experience, became king at a time when France was on the verge of political and social collapse. France required a strong and resourceful monarch to see the kingdom through such turmoil, but Henry was ostentatious and weak. Between 1574 and 1589 France suffered from four more religious wars and Henry III oversaw a disintegration of monarchical authority.

How damaging was Alençon to the French monarchy?

Huguenot nobles were always likely to target Navarre's independence as a priority for continued survival of the Huguenot cause. Alençon was a different matter. Although young and inexperienced, Alençon was beginning to attract the attention of influential and ambitious princes, known as the *politiques*, such as Navarre, Condé and de la Mole. In fact, many of these princes at court were motivated by their own ambitions to advance their careers. **Alençon's opposition** was rooted in his jealousy of Henry. He fled court in September 1575. He then issued a political manifesto from Dreux which announced his armed opposition to his brother's tyranny. Alençon then marched his small band of Catholic princes southwards to link up with the forces being assembled by Condé and **John of Casimir**. Such an alliance was extremely serious for Henry III on two counts:

- Casimir's father, Elector Frederick III of the Palatinate, had recently provided 20,000 German mercenaries for an invasion of France. Added to the Huguenot forces commanded by Condé, Damville and the recently

KEY TERMS

Politiques Describes those in favour of religious coexistence in order to ensure stability. The term was only really used after 1584, but these princes were certainly moderates and were not necessarily bound together along confessional lines.

KEY THEMES

Alençon's opposition
Alençon claimed that he opposed the King's advisers such as the Guises, not the King himself, but this did not ring true. Alençon also called for a religious peace in order that a church council could be held and for a meeting of the Estates General.

KEY PEOPLE

John of Casimir Son of Frederick III of the Palatinate, John of Casimir led a German mercenary army into France in 1576 to fight on behalf of the Huguenots.

escaped Navarre the overall Protestant army in the field outnumbered the royal forces.

- Alençon was heir to the throne and this offered the coalition rebel forces, status and legality.

What happened in the Fifth War of Religion, 1576?

Alençon was put at the forefront of negotiations with the King, and he presented a remonstrance (see page 77) of 93 articles to Henry III in March 1576. Alençon, Navarre, Damville and Condé demanded:

- the free exercise of the reformed religion
- the creation of unbiased courts where Huguenots could receive justice
- a number of fortified towns as well as payment of the German mercenaries under Casimir
- individual requests, for example Alençon asked for the title of **Duke of Anjou**.

The demands of the Huguenot princes led by the Catholic Alençon were overwhelming and almost unbelievable considering that this was only four years after St Bartholomew's Day. Yet, Henry III and Catherine de Medici were hardly in a position to refuse the remonstrance because the royal forces could not match those mustered by Condé, Navarre and Damville. With the German mercenaries under Casimir closing in on the towns of the Loire Valley, Henry III decided to give in to the demands of his brother and with barely a shot being fired the Fifth War of Religion was brought to an end with the Edict of Beaulieu on 6 May 1576. Known as the Peace of Monsieur, as it was seen to have been forced upon the King by his brother, it represented a massive turnaround in Huguenot fortunes.

What were the terms of the Peace of Monsieur?

The treaty comprised 63 articles and concessions to the Huguenots were considerable:

- All French Protestants were given the right of a free, public and general exercise of religion everywhere in France except Paris. This meant that Protestant churches could be built.

- Special law courts were established guaranteeing equality in cases involving litigants of different faiths.
- The King was to call a meeting of the Estates General within six months and the Huguenots were granted eight surety towns, mainly in the south.
- Alençon was granted the duchies and revenue of Anjou, Touraine and Berry along with an annual pension of over 300,000 livres.

The peace was met with predictable hostility from Catholics all over France. Henry had reconciled with Alençon and there were clauses in the peace which required Huguenots to restore Catholic worship in towns where it had been abolished and Protestants to observe Catholic feast days, but to many Catholics Henry appeared to have given in to Huguenot force.

Yet although the concessions were unprecedented it is crucial to remember that this treaty was dictated in arms and the long-term policies of Henry and Catherine towards the Huguenots did not change. Also, Huguenot strength was boosted by the mercenaries and financial aid of Elector Frederick, and their actual number on the ground remained less than eight per cent of the population. Finally, the leadership of Alençon and other Catholic princes gave the Huguenots greater legitimacy and ensured that Henry took their demands seriously.

Why was the Catholic League formed in 1577?

At the Estates General which opened at Blois in November 1576, the assembly was dominated by Catholic deputies opposed to the Peace of Monsieur. Most of the Catholic deputies were in favour of a return to war although few were willing to bear the financial burden demanded by Henry III. The clergy voted unanimously for the suppression of Protestantism and granted the king subsidies for this purpose. The nobility also decided in favour of religious uniformity but were eager to stress their right to be exempt from taxation. The third estate included a minority of moderates who wished for a negotiated peace and religious tolerance. Among the moderates was the legist and political theorist **Jean Bodin**, whose *Six Books of the Commonwealth* had just appeared. In the end, the third

KEY PEOPLE

Jean Bodin (1529–96)
Argued in favour of a lasting peace that would restore order to the kingdom, and he opposed the King's demands for an increase in taxation. Although an advocate of monarchical absolutism, Bodin did not believe that a rise in taxation was in the best interests of the crown because the populace had already been forced to endure fiscal strain.

estate voted for the suppression of Protestantism but hoped that it could be achieved without war.

KEY TERMS

Cahier de doléances
Complaints presented to the king by each estate at a meeting of the Estates General.

In February 1577, each estate handed over its own *cahier de doléances* which demanded the eradication of Protestantism and the restoration of Catholicism as the one true faith. Yet Henry had been granted little additional income in order to carry out this aim, and the unwillingness of the nobility and the third estate to assist the king financially severely undermined his position.

As the Huguenots were already mobilised and making ground in the regions of Provence and Dauphine, the Catholic militants at Blois became frustrated at the King's lack of action. Many of these Catholics, including Henry, Duke of Guise, had already realised that their aims and ambitions would be better served through the formation of their own party designed to defend the Catholic cause, and thus the Catholic League was born. Guise issued a manifesto proclaiming the Holy Catholic League which aimed to:

• implement the law of God in its entirety
• uphold Catholic worship
• maintain the king in the authority and obedience owed to him by his subjects.

Ultimately, the League undermined Henry's authority – a fact which he recognised in December 1576 when he tried unsuccessfully to put himself at the head of the League. Henry's aim was to deny leadership to the Guises, but as he had no money to wage a war which he had been put under pressure to renew and had subsequently started, the League lost faith in the King and his advisers whom the militants branded *mignons* (or pretty ones). Henry had managed to win back Damville from the Huguenot cause in 1577 luring him with the marquisate of Saluzzo.

What happened in the Sixth War of Religion?
The Sixth War of Religion was always likely to be brief and inconclusive given the King's lack of funding. Fighting began in December 1576 and the royal army under Anjou

and the Duke of Nevers struggled from the outset, hampered by inadequate supplies and equipment.

What were the terms of the Peace of Bergerac?

The Peace of Bergerac in 1577 halted the fighting but like all the previous settlements made little impact on the long-term prospects of peace. It limited the concessions given to the Huguenots at the Peace of Monsieur: freedom of worship was restricted to the suburbs of only one town per *bailliage* and to towns held by the Huguenots on 17 September. Catholic worship was to be restored throughout the kingdom and all leagues and confraternities were to be banned. The Peace of Bergerac was very much Henry III's peace; a belated attempt to restore royal authority.

What happened in the Seventh War of Religion, 1577–80?

Between 1577 and 1580, the Peace of Bergerac was threatened by continuing tensions in the Low Countries. Moreover, Henry III's credibility as king of France continued to be eroded as both Protestants and Catholics openly flouted the recent peace edict. **Unrest at court** continued between Henry's supporters and other courtiers such as Guise and Anjou.

Amid peasant uprisings in the south-east over increased fiscal burdens, and the ambitious foreign policy of Anjou in the Netherlands the seventh and shortest war of religion, nicknamed the **Lovers' War**, broke out in the north. Most Huguenots in the Midi were not in favour of a costly and long war, and Anjou was more interested in furthering his own cause in the Netherlands.

The effects of war on the civilian populations was devastating as can be seen in this petition to the King written in 1579:

> *The insolence, authority and power of the seigneurs, captains and soldiers has been the cause of great misery. The local folk have suffered at their hands and I relay their miseries and grievances to Your Majesty… they had been buried alive in heaps of manure, thrown into wells and ditches and left to die howling like dogs: they*

Peasant revolts, 1579.

had been nailed in boxes without air, walled up in towers without food, and garrotted upon trees in the depths of the mountains and forests; they had been stretched in front of fires, their feet fricasseed in grease; their women had been raped and those who were pregnant aborted; their children had been kidnapped and ransomed, or even roasted alive before the parents... there had been burnings, ransoms, sackings, levies, tailles and tolls together with seizures of goods, grain and livestock. In one year impositions placed upon them first by Catholic and then by Protestant garrisons had exceeded the amount of the taille in the last thirty years.

In as much as the seigneurs of the said region together with their officers have permitted and do continue to permit infinite crimes and excesses, and do shelter and defend the murderers, robbers and disturbers of public

*peace may it please Your Majesty to command and
enjoin most expressly that they must abstain from
withdrawing the above named into their houses.*

What were the terms of the Peace of Felix?

Another compromise peace settlement was arranged in
November 1580. Existing Protestant political and religious
privileges were acknowledged between Navarre and Anjou,
and the Huguenots were allowed to keep their surety towns
for a further six years. Such a settlement was as doomed to
fail just as the previous six edicts had been. Henry had
once more lacked adequate funds and resources to defeat
the Huguenots and his situation was made worse by the
increasing popularity of Guise and the actions of his
brother Anjou, who proved a complete liability both in life
and in death.

WHY WAS ANJOU A CONTINUING THREAT TO THE MONARCHY?

Though he had abandoned the Huguenots after the peace
of Monsieur, **Anjou's activities** still commanded attention
from Protestant governments' abroad. He was again being
touted as a potential husband for the English Queen
Elizabeth I, in 1577. More worrying for Henry III was his
brother's contacts with the Dutch rebels. The Dutch
Calvinist provinces of Holland and Zeeland were interested
in using Anjou as a sovereign figurehead to replace Philip
II of Spain as their prince. Henry III was eager to see a
decline in Spanish domination of the Netherlands, but he
was anxious not to go to war with Philip. Anjou's blatant
support for the Dutch rebels in July 1578 when he arrived
in Mons and offered his assistance to William of Orange
threatened Franco-Spanish neutrality. Fears of a Spanish
reprisal were temporarily put on hold, however, as Anjou's
aid vanished amid the ill discipline and disorganisation of
his troops. Nevertheless, in 1580 Anjou signed another
agreement with the Dutch rebels at Plessis les Tours:

- It installed the Duke as successor to Philip II as
  sovereign prince in the seven northern provinces which
  were revolting against Spanish rule.

- Anjou was to receive a sizeable annual pension as well as various titles in return for French military aid and leadership.
- The Dutch States-General were vigilant, however, in terms of placing limitations on Anjou's power. Anjou had no authority over the army or in deciding the religion of each province. Even with such checks on his power the fact remained that Anjou was openly assisting the Dutch rebels in their fight against Spain.

In 1582, Anjou was installed as prince and lord of the Dutch provinces in the north. Reliant upon funding from his brother and Elizabeth I, Anjou made little impact upon the Spanish army in the Netherlands. Frustrated by checks on his sovereign power and with the Dutch falling behind on his annual stipend, Anjou became disillusioned with his role in the northern provinces. In 1583, he lost the support of the Dutch after his army tried to seize Antwerp by force and he was forced to return to France.

Why was the death of Anjou a key turning point for the French monarchy?
On 10 June 1584, the Duke of Anjou died of tuberculosis at his estate in Château Thierry. The implications of his death for the French crown were enormous because Henry III had no son. For some time most Catholics had believed that Anjou would succeed his elder brother. The death of Anjou left Henry of Navarre as heir under **Salic law**. The implications of the Huguenot leader Navarre becoming king of France were unthinkable for most Frenchmen, who believed in the **Catholicity of the crown**, and opposition from militant Catholics was inevitable and fierce. Navarre refused an invitation from Henry III to abjure his faith for a second time, possibly fearing for his life if he came to court. With Navarre next in line to the throne, the intensity and bloodshed of the French Wars of Religion grew worse throughout the remainder of the 1580s.

What was the impact of Anjou's death on the Catholic League?
Henry of Navarre's proximity to the throne filled most Catholics with sheer horror and prompted Henry, Duke of Guise to revitalise the Catholic Holy Union established at

the Estates General at Blois in 1576. The stakes now were very much higher, and Guise relished the opportunity to take the limelight and advance his own status as leader of the League. In September 1584, Guise and his two brothers, the Duke of Mayenne and the Cardinal of Guise, along with two other nobles founded an institution specifically designed to keep Navarre off the French throne.

In December 1584, the Catholic League signed a treaty with Philip II at Joinville which agreed on the aim of defending the Catholic faith, removing Protestantism from France and the Netherlands and recognising that a heretic could not become king. The agreement suited both parties:

- For the Guises it brought power and wealth to the League because Philip agreed to pay a monthly subsidy of 50,000 escudos in order for it to wage war against the Huguenots.
- For Philip it brought the opportunity to interfere in French affairs, undermine Henry III and promote and publish the decrees of the Council of Trent which the French crown had refused to register. Potential territorial gains for Philip at Cambrai and along the Spanish border were relatively unimportant in comparison with the chance to dictate League policy in France.

Where did support for the League come from?

The League itself existed on a number of levels and accordingly drew on a range of social classes for support:

- At the top came the Guises who had a vast clientele network among the aristocracy throughout Lorraine, Champagne, Burgundy and Brittany where their interests were strongly represented. Together this noble group provided military and political direction.
- The popular arm of the organisation existed in urban centres where merchants, the urban gentry and artisans provided the membership. Predictably the urban leagues were more fundamental and intense in their policies. This was especially true in Paris where the revolutionary committee known as the **Sixteen**, after the sixteen *quartiers* of the city, was established.

The Sixteen Founded by a group of urban notables, in the beginning it was the domain of the middle classes. Yet even at this early stage the Sixteen enjoyed widespread popular support because of its commitment to eradicate Protestantism and keep the crown Catholic. The Sixteen soon evolved to become a powerful political body, independent of Guise control and revolutionary in nature.

The League was a complex institution which was only loosely under Guise control. The one issue which bound it together was protection of the Catholic faith. At Reims in March 1585, the League issued a public manifesto outlining its **aims and objectives**. The tone of the manifesto was a highly critical one towards Henry III and Catherine de Medici for having tolerated Protestantism for so long, and having placed a huge fiscal burden on the populace. In 1576, Henry III had sought wisely to put himself at the head of the League, but he was in no position to sideline Guise. Instead Henry III was forced to submit to the League through the **Treaty of Nemours** in July 1585. All Huguenot gains since the start of the Wars of Religion were essentially revoked, and two months later Pope Sixtus V excommunicated Navarre and Condé. Both were now barred from the succession. Nemours demonstrates how low royal authority had become, as Henry III had little option but to capitulate before the League at Nemours given his precarious financial position.

What happened in the Eighth War of Religion?

Unsurprisingly, the terms of Nemours and the League's alliance with Spain sparked a renewal of violence in late 1585, as Catholic nobles set about enforcing Nemours. The death of Anjou had initiated the War of the Three Henrys – the King, Navarre and Guise. The Eighth War lasted for more than a decade and witnessed more bloodshed than any of the previous conflicts.

The initiative for the Catholic attack in northern and eastern France came from the League rather than the King. With Philip II's subsidy and the full backing of the Guises along with popular support, the League found itself in a stronger situation than the crown to deal with Protestantism. The Huguenots, appalled by the Treaty of Nemours (apparently half of Navarre's moustache turned white on hearing of its terms), looked once more to Germany and England for support. The Queen of England gave 100,000 crowns to the reformed cause and Casimir once more mobilised mercenaries in the Palatinate.

Henry III momentarily placated Catholic opinion by registering a series of anti-Huguenot edicts, but in the long term the militants demanded action and Henry was unable to offer his generals sufficient resources to crush Condé and Navarre. Catholic opinion was further intensified by news of the **execution of Mary, Queen of Scots**, and many wanted Henry to avenge her death. Henry's control of the kingdom was slowly slipping away, and rumours of League-inspired plots to kidnap the King and seize power were commonplace throughout the spring of 1586.

On the battlefield, the Catholic aim was to repel the German mercenaries under Casimir which had crossed the border into eastern France. A leaguer army under Guise confronted the Germans while a royal force under the Duke of Joyeuse marched south to meet Navarre's forces and prevent them from linking up with the mercenaries. The Huguenots defeated the royal forces at Coutras in October 1587 and killed Joyeuse in the process. The victory was offset however by a crushing defeat inflicted by Guise on the Germans outside Chartres. In early 1588, two of Navarre's allies, Henry, Prince of Condé, and Robert de la Marck, Duke of Bouillon, died, leaving Navarre as sole leader of Huguenot forces. Catholic forces seemed to be in the ascendency, but disunity between leaguers and royalists prevented outright victory. Henry III further angered Henry of Guise by awarding his royal favourite, the **Duke of Epernon**, with offices previously held by Joyeuse. Moreover those who supported Henry III were now labelled in a rather derisory fashion as *politiques*. Soon the minority of *politiques* became bitter enemies of the Sixteen, who increasingly looked to Guise for inspiration.

How far did the League undermine royal authority?

In early 1588, tension between Guise and the King increased as the League made a series of demands to Henry III which included the dismissal of Epernon, the acceptance of Guise's policy in exterminating heresy and publication of the decrees of the Council of Trent. Attempts were made on Epernon's life by those leaguers who resented his political influence on the King and his fortune. In April 1588, Henry III prohibited Duke Henry of Guise from entering Paris. When Guise defied the ban and entered the capital in May to a tumultuous welcome from the Sixteen and other Parisian Catholics, a showdown between two of the three Henrys was inevitable.

KEY EVENTS

Execution of Mary, Queen of Scots Having fled to England in 1568 after defeat at the Battle of Langside, Mary was imprisoned by Elizabeth. Her presence in England gave rise to countless plots to depose Elizabeth and restore Catholicism. Finally, after the Babington Conspiracy in 1586, she was brought to trial for treason and executed at Fotheringhay Castle, Northamptonshire.

KEY PEOPLE

Duke of Epernon (1554–1642) Became governor of Normandy and admiral of France, while Guise, the conqueror of Casimir's mercenaries, received nothing. Leaguer propaganda tore into Epernon who was accused of building up his own fortune at the expense of the kingdom.

KEY EVENTS

The Day of the Barricades According to Mack Holt, the events in Paris on 12 May 1588 marked the nadir of royal authority in Henry III's reign. The king was no longer resident in his capital.

KEY EVENTS

Advancement of the Sixteen Thirteen of the sixteen colonels of the city militia were replaced while the leader of the Sixteen, La Chapelle Marteau, was elected as mayor and in the process swore an oath of loyalty to Guise and the cardinal of Bourbon.

KEY EVENTS

The Edict of Union, 1588 Henry was forced to dismiss Epernon, reaffirm the Treaty of Nemours, recognise the Cardinal of Bourbon as heir to the throne, appoint Guise lieutenant-general of the realm (commander-in-chief of the army) and call a meeting of the Estates General for the autumn in order to prepare for all-out war against the Huguenots.

Guise had defied the King in entering Paris in the first place, but tried to justify his conduct in terms of meeting the King and possibly negotiating a settlement. On the **Day of the Barricades**, Henry III chose not to have Guise arrested but instead posted over 4,000 Swiss guards in strategic positions around the city. Parisians objected to the presence of the Swiss and rumours spread of another royal massacre but this time with Catholics as the victims. Parisians from every social level took up arms against the royal troops while streets and neighbourhoods were cordoned off and protected with barricades formed by stretching chains across street corners:

- With the capital clearly behind the League, Henry had little option but to leave Paris. On 13 May, he fled to Chartres and on the following day the Bastille surrendered to Guise.
- The King's supporters fled the city and were replaced in official posts by more radical officers loyal to the League and the Sixteen. Effectively a coup d'état had occurred and as a result Henry III had lost control of his capital.

With the gates of the city secure and the militia purged much power had actually passed over to the ordinary populace. A new revolutionary government may have provisionally been in place in 1588, but just how much control **the Sixteen** and Guise exercised in the absence of the King is questionable. Certainly the capital was about to experience a period of radical government.

What happened in the Edict of Union, 1588?

Meanwhile, Henry III's humiliation was completed in a new **Edict of Union** (July 1588) which reflected his loss of authority. Henry looked to play for time, all the while plotting revenge on his rivals. Buoyed by news of the failure of Philip II's Armada against England, Henry sacked his ministers and replaced them with younger, more independent-minded men who, importantly, owed nothing to Catherine de Medici. Men such as Francois d'O and Montholon entered the king's service and Catherine's influence in political affairs dwindled. Although Henry could control appointments to his own council he could not influence elections for the Estates General and all three presidents were leading leaguers. The financial problems of the King left him vulnerable and exposed to criticism. Salaries of office holders remained unpaid while annuities were also outstanding. Henry had to agree to the creation of a financial tribunal to oversee fiscal affairs while the third estate took this opportunity to question the nature of royal authority. No doubt the third estate were being encouraged by aristocratic leaguers to undermine the position of the King further, but for once Henry III was ready to respond in ruthless fashion.

Why did the King murder the Duke and Cardinal of Guise?

In an act of calculated desperation, Henry III decided to strike at the heart of the League and avenge his recent disgrace. On 23 December 1588, he summoned the Duke and Cardinal of Guise to his apartments in the Château of Blois, where the royal guards immediately **murdered the Duke** and arrested his brother the Cardinal. The following day, as the King was in Mass for Christmas, the Cardinal of Guise was killed while other prominent leaguers were imprisoned, including the Cardinal of Bourbon.

What were the consequences of Guises' murders?

Resistance to Henry in Paris intensified. A Guise cousin, the Duke of Aumale, became governor of Paris and the League's Council of Forty named the youngest Guise brother (Charles, Duke of Mayenne) lieutenant-general of the realm. The new council denounced Henry III as tyrannical and the Sorbonne declared the King deposed and called upon all Frenchmen to rise against him in defence of the Catholic faith. If the death of Anjou had sparked debate on the Catholicity of the crown, the murder of the Guises provoked an explosion of League radicalism.

On 5 January 1589, Catherine de Medici died. This removed the one person who may have been able to negotiate with the Catholic militants. Subsequently, Henry was more vulnerable and isolated than ever. He controlled much of the Loire as well as Bordeaux; to the north the League was dominant; to the south the Huguenots were in command. Henry desperately needed an ally for both

KEY EVENTS

The murder of Guise
Henry claimed that he acted in self-defence and that the Guises were plotting to murder and depose him. However, few believed him and news of the murders spread quickly, sparking off feelings of grief, resentment and anger in the towns loyal to the League.

KEY THEMES

Resistance to Henry The most persuasive and powerful advocate of authorised regicide was Jean Boucher, a parish priest of Saint Benoît and a leading light in the administration of Paris from 1589. Boucher published his views in a tract *De Justa Henrici tertii abdicatione* (Just Deposition of Henry III) in which Henry was charged with ten major crimes. Boucher called upon the Pope to release Henry's subjects from their obedience and, failing this, the people must depose and kill the despot.

Catholic propagandists advocated murdering Henry, arguing that kingship was a human institution created by the people for their own convenience. Sovereignty had been transferred to the king in a contract between God and the people. The people retained power over the king in order to ensure that the contract was observed and fulfilled. In short, the monarchy was elective, the people held sovereign power and tyrannical kings could be deposed legitimately by force.

EXAM TIPS

The Catholic League is an important institution on a religious and a political level.

Use the League in an essay on:

- The Monarchy – to show how important the sacred, Catholic nature of the crown was and what happened when that principle came under threat. Its creation highlights the decline in monarchical power as the League was headed by Guise and funded by Philip II.
- The Nobility – to show how powerful leading nobles could become when the monarchy was weak. The succession crisis galvanised and radicalised the catholic nobility.
- Religion – to show how it continued to fuel violence in the 1580s. The league was based on fundamental Gallican values.
- Society – to show the broad base of support for the League that existed on different levels within Paris and why it eventually self destructed.

military and financial purposes. In reality, he had only one remaining option: to seek an alliance with Navarre.

On 30 April, Henry III and Henry of Navarre signed an alliance at Plessis les Tours which involved the King recognising Navarre as his rightful successor. The two combined armies marched on the capital capturing Senlis and Pontoise on the way. A major clash with the Catholic forces seemed inevitable and within Paris anti-Valois passions reached fever pitch. Henry was portrayed as the Antichrist in **League propaganda** and calls for his assassination grew louder.

As the king's forces besieged Paris in August 1589, a young Dominican lay brother named Jacques Clément made his way into the royal camp intent on carrying out his duty to God and kill Henry. Clément bluffed his way into the camp saying that he carried a message of support from the King's supporters still in Paris. The King beckoned him closer at which point Clément stabbed Henry in the abdomen. The King died the following day and the Valois dynasty was over. Before he died, Henry had declared Navarre to be his heir on the condition that he converted to Catholicism. Salic law endorsed the late King's proclamation yet with no conversion imminent and Navarre being a convinced Huguenot the troubles were far from over.

News of the King's assassination prompted rejoicing in the capital and Clément was subsequently canonised by the League convinced as they were that outright Catholic triumph was close at hand.

CHAPTER SUMMARY: WHAT WAS THE CATHOLIC LEAGUE?

- The Catholic League was a Holy Union made up of the middle/working class urban element and the noble Guise cohort.
- It originated in opposition to the Peace of Monsieur (1576) but really came to the fore in 1584 after the death of Anjou.
- The League was united by a desire to keep the crown Catholic.

- As the King wavered, the League gained in popularity which led to the Day of the Barricades in 1588.
- The League supported the claims to the throne of the Cardinal of Bourbon (and others after his death) rather than Navarre.

Why is the Catholic League important?
- It demonstrates how important the Catholicity of the Crown was to Catholic French nobility.
- It highlights the split that was emerging from within the Catholic noble faction between moderate royalists and radical leaguers leading to the 'War of the Three Henrys' (Guise, Navarre and the King).
- It shows the weakness of the crown as the League dictated policy to the King. Henry III was not financially strong enough to stand up to this Catholic institution.
- The Treaty of Nemours of 1585 should be viewed as a capitulation by the crown to the League as all former edicts of pacification were revoked and the reformed religion was outlawed. This was repeated in 1588 after the Day of the Barricades with the Edict of Union. The Cardinal of Bourbon was recognised as the rightful heir to the throne.
- The League attempted to do what the Crown could not: win the war against the Huguenots.
- To defeat the League, in 1588, Henry III murdered the Guises and allied with Henry of Navarre. This would have been unthinkable ten years previously.
- At an urban level the League is represented by the Sixteen in Paris who become increasingly radical and militant. The split between the noble and urban Leagues develops.

The specification key themes across the period can be summarised as follows:

Nation state
The emergence of the Catholic League under the leadership of Philip II undermines the concept of national unity and perhaps shows us that religious loyalties come before national ones. Frenchmen are willing to support the King of Spain in order to keep a Protestant off the throne. The longer term trend of ongoing civil conflict continues to pull power away from the centre and towards the localities, thus undermining the concept of nation state.

Relations between kings and subjects

This period (1574–89) marks the low point of monarchical authority and relations between the king and his subjects are never worse. Huguenot nobility continue to challenge Henry III's right to rule, whilst Guise leadership of the Catholic League in association with Spain undermines monarchical power on the Catholic side. When Catholic resistance theories begin to emerge after the Guise murders, one can point to the nadir of royal authority in France. At a lower level, the impact of civil war on local communities begins to take its toll, demonstrated by frequent peasant unrest.

Religious developments

Whilst the conflict becomes increasingly politicised through factional strife and foreign involvement, the heart of the struggle remains religious. The popularity of the League in this period lies in its vow to maintain the catholicity of the French crown. The unpopularity of the Crown remains its inability to expel heresy from France.

Social and economic developments

The impact of over twenty-five years of civil war on the population of France has pushed the peasantry to breaking point. Marauding armies and forced billeting have ruined agricultural productivity and created misery and hardship in the countryside. The longevity and intensity of the French Wars of Religion meant that virtually all of France was affected by the conflict. Still, a few areas such as Nantes and La Rochelle continued to see economic growth even in this chaotic period as they benefited from the shift in trade from the Mediterranean to the Atlantic.

QUESTIONS TO CONSIDER

1. Why did successive peace edicts fail to keep the peace?

2. How were the Huguenots able to wage war effectively after St Bartholomew's Day?

3. In what ways did the Catholic League undermine the authority of the crown?

4. To what extent was Henry III a failure as king of France?

CHAPTER 8

The triumph of Henry IV, 1589–98

The assassination of Henry III and the resulting power vacuum polarised opinion in France and divided the realm:

- The *parlement*s under pressure from the League immediately recognised the Cardinal of Bourbon (still imprisoned) as King Charles X.
- The Protestants recognised Navarre as Henry IV.
- The Catholic army at Saint Cloud, which had been part of the unlikely alliance between the late King and Navarre, was split. Many decided to join the League, and radicals such as La Trémoille immediately withdrew their forces from the camp at Meudon. The royal army besieging Paris halved in number as many refused to serve a 'heretical' king thus ensuring that the siege failed.
- However, Catholic captains led by François d'O recognised Navarre as king on his acceptance of an accord in which Navarre promised to protect the Catholic faith, and place towns and fortresses seized from the rebels under Catholic control while still guaranteeing Protestant rights in areas that they held.

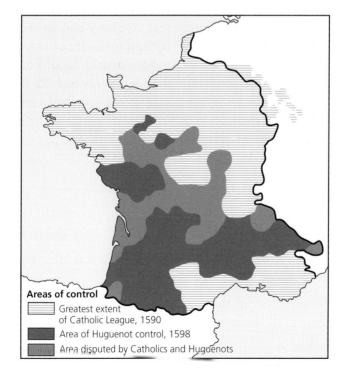

Areas of control

Greatest extent of Catholic League, 1590

Area of Huguenot control, 1598

Area disputed by Catholics and Huguenots

Areas of League and Huguenot control.

HOW DID HENRY OF NAVARRE BECOME KING?

It was not going to be an easy task for Henry to convince Catholic France that he was fit to be their king. Never before had a Protestant succeeded to the throne. Leaguer nobles in particular were likely to put up a determined fight to keep Navarre off the throne. Spanish aid would bolster their defiance. Yet, by 1598 Navarre had managed to assert himself as the legitimate king of France. As we shall see, this was achieved through a mixture of political skill, pragmatism, force and good fortune.

1. Appeasement

Already it was clear that the new king-elect faced a daunting task. On the one hand, he recognised that if he was to succeed to the throne he required the support of the moderate Catholic majority who were becoming increasingly tired of civil war. Such support would only come at the price of his rejection of Protestantism. On the other hand, this move would upset the Huguenots. Henry did his best to satisfy both camps:

- An immediate religious conversion was out of the question but he obtained the support of royal Catholic officials, both secular and clerical with his broad commitment to a Catholic monarchy and realm.
- To many moderate Catholics, support for Henry was preferable to that for the League because at least this would keep Gallican independence from Rome alive.

2. Military action

Alongside the policy of appeasement Henry recognised the need for effective military action and force in order to defeat the League on the battlefield.

- In September 1589, Henry was victorious over the Duke of Mayenne at **Arques** near Dieppe.
- Henry followed up victory at Arques with further successes throughout Normandy. In the winter of 1589, all major towns except Rouen and Le Havre were taken and, in March 1590, Mayenne's army was routed once again at Ivry.

- Paris, however, proved to be a real obstacle for Henry, galvanised as it was by the Duke of Nemours, who had supplanted the hapless Mayenne as commander of the League. Between May and September 1590, Henry's siege brought great hardship and death to the citizens of the capital with Henry himself well aware that his activities might unite Catholic opinion against him. However, as Henry called off the siege in September, events conspired to work in his favour.

3. Lack of a creditable alternative

In May 1590, the Cardinal of Bourbon had died and in September, Mayenne claimed the throne for himself. Most Leaguers preferred Mayenne's younger nephew Charles, Duke of Guise, while others advocated the accession of Philip II of Spain in order to save the faith.

In short, the extreme Catholic faction was disunited in their views over who should become king, and to the majority of people in France, Henry was gradually emerging as the only reasonable claimant.

4. Support for the Sixteen and the League wanes

Furthermore, the group of Sixteen was becoming too powerful, resulting in division between the noble League led by Mayenne and the revolutionary government in the capital:

- In late 1590, the Sixteen embarked upon a campaign of terror directed against anyone suspected of moderate or *politiques* views.
- The *parlement* protested and several members of the Sixteen resigned. The new, more radical Sixteen made up of La Chapelle-Marteau, Acarie and Bussy-Leclerc were determined to stamp out any royalist sympathisers.
- Paranoia took over and *parlement* was accused of being too lenient over its action towards a royal agent Brigard.
- On 15 November 1591, the Sixteen purged the *parlement*, executing its president Barnabé Brisson in the process. Two other magistrates suffered the same fate and it appeared that the capital was being governed by fear and terror. Mayenne was forced to march back into Paris

and restore order by force, with the result that four of the Sixteen were hanged at the Louvre.

Whether the Sixteen was representative of the lower classes and popular opinion is highly debatable. However, it is clear that divisions between those who opposed Henry of Navarre were widening. Support for the League and the Sixteen had reached its pinnacle during the Day of the Barricades when opposition to Henry III had united Parisians. In 1591, other issues such as Spanish intervention, the succession, the nature of royal authority and the fear of social disorder served to polarise opinion and the role of the Sixteen waned considerably, much to the advantage of Henry of Navarre.

5. War weariness and the presence of Spanish troops on French soil

Henry IV's sieges of Paris (1590) and Rouen (1592) failed because of one of Philip II's leading generals, the Duke of Parma. Despite numerical and financial advantages, Parma was unable to inflict an outright defeat on Henry IV. Moreover, just before the siege of Rouen Henry had audaciously launched an offensive with some 7,000 cavalry against the 23,000-strong Spanish force, led by Parma at Aumale. Parma ordered his men to withdraw, certain that Henry must have reserves capable of inflicting a serious defeat on the Spanish. Henry had no such reserves and clearly risked disaster at Aumale. Yet his gamble paid off and thereafter he avoided open warfare. A period of stalemate ensued in which divisions within the League became more apparent and a combination of the presence of Spanish troops on French soil, tiredness with war, pillaging troops and poor harvests combined to present strong government under Henry IV as an attractive option.

6. Bribery

Henry spent around 30 million livres in bribes and often he agreed to settle a town's debts or exempt it from tax as compensation for the ravages of war. Such actions were good examples of Henry's pragmatism in the wake of the Wars of Religion and his recognition that urban and noble support were crucial to his kingship.

7. Henry becomes a Catholic

In 1593, Mayenne summoned an Estates General to Paris in order to resolve the question of succession:

- The Spanish ambassador proposed a **Spanish succession** of Philip II's daughter – the Infanta Isabella Clara Eugenia, grand-daughter of Henry II, but barred from succession by Salic law which prevented a woman succeeding to the throne.
- It was Henry IV who broke the deadlock when he announced his decision to abandon the reformed faith. On 25 July 1593, he solemnly abjured in the abbey at Saint Denis. Henry's conversion was a critical turning point in the French Wars of Religion because at once Henry removed the League's main reason for excluding him from the succession. While he may not have been a genuine Catholic to the extremists; Henry's conversion was what many of the more moderate *politiques* Catholics had been waiting for.
- Town governors now saw it appropriate to declare their loyalty to Henry although such capitulation did not come cheaply and bribes were used to win over Leaguer towns and nobles. Agreements included clauses forbidding Protestant worship and leaguer office holders retained their positions. Thus, Henry continued his policy of appeasement towards towns of the League, a far cheaper and more attractive alternative to war.

8. The coronation ceremony

On 27 February 1594, Henry was crowned at Chartres rather than the customary Reims, which was still in the hands of the League. Nevertheless, the usual pomp and ceremony accompanied his coronation and, importantly, Henry swore the coronation oath promising to expel all heretics from his kingdom. On 22 March, Henry entered Paris, meeting with little resistance, and symbolically, heard Mass at Notre Dame.

9. Conciliation with Rome

In September 1595, he reached an agreement with Pope Clement VIII promising to publish the decrees of the Council of Trent in return for absolution. With the Sorbonne, *parlements*, papacy and most importantly the

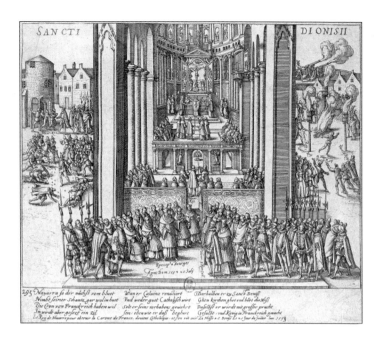

majority of the populace behind him, Henry could now
turn his attention towards ridding France of the Spanish.

10. War with Spain

War was declared on Spain in January 1595 and in June of
that year a royalist force led by Henry himself defeated the
numerically superior Spanish at Fontaine-Francaise. Henry
had won Burgundy and subsequently entered Lyons.
Mayenne was disillusioned with his Spanish allies and came
over to the King's side. Guise, Epernon and Joyeuse
followed suit in early 1596 and of the great, influential
nobles, only the Duke of Mercouer remained aloof.

- By September 1596, Amiens had fallen to Henry and by
  the end of the year Mercouer had submitted to the
  King's authority also.
- All the great nobles were suitably compensated for their
  actions and by the spring of 1598 the situation was
  considerably better for Henry than it had been a year
  previously.
- Despite inevitable discontent and resentment from the
  Protestant minority which manifested itself in assemblies
  at Sainte Foy (1594), Saumur (1595) and Loudun
  (1596) all factions were ready to listen to peace terms at
  Nantes in 1595.

TO WHAT EXTENT DID THE EDICT OF NANTES (13 APRIL 1598) RESOLVE THE RELIGIOUS DISPUTE?

The Edict of Nantes provided a legal and political structure for ending the Wars of Religion although the actual process was never going to be quick or easy. The edict consisted of four separate documents: the 92 general articles, the 56 secret articles and two royal **brevets**. The 92 articles generally reaffirmed the provisions of earlier edicts:

- They recognised the legal existence of the French reformed churches and granted Protestants the same civil rights as Catholics.
- Huguenots were free to acquire or inherit office and bipartisan courts (*chambres mi parties*) were established in the *parlement*s to judge lawsuits involving Protestants.
- However, Huguenots were still not allowed to impose taxes, build fortifications, levy troops or hold political assemblies.
- Moreover, Protestant worship was still a contentious issue; to be allowed in two places in each *bailliage* and wherever the Huguenots could prove it had been openly practised in 1596 and 1597.

Henry's pragmatism was displayed in the edict in which Catholics and Protestants could live together in peace, despite the fact that Protestantism had not been given full parity with Catholicism:

- The 56 secret articles appeased certain towns with specific promises to ensure the safe passage of the edict through the *parlement*s. Paris and Toulouse for example did not have to tolerate Protestant worship inside their walls while commissioners were also appointed to ensure that the edict was carried out on the ground.
- The two brevets were the most significant part of the edict in many ways. In them, Protestants were granted a degree of military and political independence establishing surety towns garrisoned by troops where Protestants could worship freely. Moreover the payment of stipends to Protestant pastors from public funds was provided and Huguenots were allowed to hold all towns

which they occupied in August 1597 for eight years. Annual royal payments were to be made to garrisons.

What was the reaction of the parlements to the Edict of Nantes?

Opposition to the Edict of Nantes was stiff among *parlementaires* and it required much pressure from Henry himself to have the edict ratified by the *parlements*. The edict was not innovative in any respect: it was based on toleration and conciliation. However, Henry IV had made it clear that the state's well-being rested on religious unity in the long term, a promise which was readily accepted by the *parlements*. Moreover, the context of the edict was very different to its predecessors in that war-weariness encouraged both sides to accept it as a lasting truce. In some respects the provisions of the edict contained the seeds of future conflict:

- The brevets had effectively created a Huguenot state within a state funded by the crown. The Huguenots were bound by royal favour but also had time, space and money to build churches and fortify towns.
- Naturally, tensions between the crown and the Huguenots came to the fore again after the death of Henry IV in 1610.

WHAT WERE THE ECONOMIC AND SOCIAL CONSEQUENCES OF THE FRENCH WARS OF RELIGION?

In general, the French Wars of Religion caused great distress throughout the kingdom: the wars between 1585 and 1596 inflicted particularly harsh suffering on millions of people. Yet throughout Europe people were experiencing economic depression brought about by population growth, land shortage and inflation. Harvest failures throughout the 1580s and 1590s caused famine across France and indeed Europe. So France would have suffered economic changes whether civil war had broken out or not. The wars made the economic crisis worse and also brought the threat of violence and disorder to French civilians:

- Mortality figures were high throughout France in the 1580s and 1590s because of harvest failure, famine and plague. Yet in areas such as Rouen it was long sieges and open warfare that raised the death toll. Moreover, while poor harvests could send prices rocketing skywards it should not be forgotten that sieges and billeting could also lead to a scarcity of resources. Paris, Rouen and La Rochelle all suffered siege warfare during this period and prices reflected this disruption. Rural economies were also affected during the civil wars as peasants suffered at the hands of billeted troops. Livestock was seized, crops requisitioned and agricultural output dropped.

- The tax demands of the crown increased throughout the period, and it was the third estate that bore the burden of the King's demands. Discontent at the increase in the level of the *taille* occasionally manifested itself in open revolt as was the case in Provence (1578), the Rhône Valley (1579) and **Normandy**. For the desperate peasant oppressed by the local landlord, economic concerns and the instinct for survival surpassed confessional allegiance. As the wars of the League took their toll, more open revolts occurred. Peasants in Brittany also revolted in 1589, targeting châteaux and other symbols of aristocratic oppression. Only in November 1590 were the peasants crushed by royalist forces at Cahaix. Even more serious uprisings occurred in Burgundy (1594 and 1597) and most famously in the south-west (by the *croquants*, 1593–95).

The Dordogne Valley regions of Limousin and Périgord suffered more than most during the Wars of Religion through billeting and bloodshed. It was here that peasants joined together in hatred of oppression. As many as 40,000 peasants assembled in Perigord in May 1594 and they appealed to the new King Henry IV to redress their grievances. The King took a sympathetic line towards them and the arrears that they owed in taxes were reduced while future levies were significantly curtailed. Henry also called for no aristocratic reprisal killings and it is likely that the *croquants* made the King aware of the need for peace at all costs. Therefore, fiscal pressures on the third estate caused many to borrow heavily from local nobles who charged exorbitant rates of interest. Economic distress and suffering

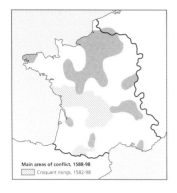

Main areas of conflict, 1588-98
Croquant risings, 1582-98

KEY THEMES

Decline in the power and status of the rural nobility The historian M.P. Holt has shown in his book *The French Wars of Religion, 1562–1629* (1995) that we must be careful with figures detailing the demise of the rural nobility. While many lesser nobles were hit hard by fiscal pressures and rapid inflation other larger landowners actually profited from the wars and it was this latter group that bought much of the available land.

were commonplace and the economic effects of the wars lasted long after the Edict of Nantes.

How did the Wars of Religion affect the nobility?

Land sale figures seem to display a **decline in the power and status of the rural nobility**, a change which some have chosen to interpret as the beginning of a decline in the political power of the nobility in France. However, great nobles benefited from Henry IV's generous policy. The powerful landowning nobles became richer and more powerful at the expense of some lesser rural nobles – hardly a fundamental shift in the makeup of society. Venality continued to enlarge the nobility of the robe (see page 18) and, while real political power and influence tended to lie with the great nobles, more individuals claiming to be of noble birth existed in France by 1600. Inter-marriage between new and old nobility further integrated the new additions and the nobility as an institution remained a healthy and vibrant political force. If anything, the gap between rich and poor grew ever wider during the Wars of Religion and it continued to be the third estate that suffered most.

CHAPTER SUMMARY: FRANCE AND THE WARS OF RELIGION 1562–98

- Calvinism never really fulfilled the promise of the 1550s and 1560s in terms of expansion and numbers of adherents. At no time did Calvinists exceed ten per cent of the population and, while a skeletal framework of national and regional synods was constructed, the notion of a national Church remained vague.
- The survival of the reformed faith through disasters such as St Bartholomew's Day and the formation of the Spanish-backed League illustrate the importance of noble protection as well as the discipline and organisation of a committed minority.
- Religion permeated every aspect of the wars. At the highest level, it shaped the peace settlements and provided the rationale for the Catholic League. At a popular level, religion incited the massacres of 1572 and

ensured that the peace edicts would fail. Throughout the period the majority of the French population stuck to the Gallican principles of one king, one faith and one law. This bond explains why toleration of a Huguenot minority was unacceptable.

- The economic impact of over 40 years of warfare was great, but ought to be viewed in the context of a general Europe-wide depression. France suffered more than most due to the cost of war although the social framework remained largely unchanged. The financial weakness of the crown undermined the rule of Henry III and explains why he was unable to defeat the Huguenots on the battlefield and subsequently became a puppet of the League.
- Political considerations were never far from the surface during the Wars of Religion as we can see from the actions of Alençon, the featuring of the Huguenot nobility in all of the peace edicts and the appeasement of major League nobles by Henry IV. Nevertheless we could argue that politics may have guided the course of the wars at times but it was religion that formed the basis of the conflict.

The specification key themes across the period can be summarised as follows:

Nation state

Henry IV's abjuration and subsequent military victory over the League, re-established the principle of strong monarchy, and began a period of political and economic recovery. The foundation stones of peace and stability were once more in place, allowing France to progress slowly towards nationhood. In the short term, the declaration of war on Spain and the expulsion of Spanish troops from French soil helped to engender a sense of national identity.

Relations between the king and his subjects

The population were becoming war weary and readily accepted Henry's abjuration as sincere on the grounds that it might bring a halt to the fighting. Henry IV was astute in buying off former Leaguer nobles, and restoring relations between the crown and the nobility in the process. The third estate were just happy with some respite in the fighting though it would take some time for France to recover from the impact of over thirty years of civil war.

Religious developments

The Edict of Nantes heralded a period of peace in France, but it did not solve all of the religious problems. A sizeable Huguenot minority, protected by the state, continued to exist, although the principle of religious unity had been re-established. Henry had recognised that only under Catholicism could peace and stability be restored to France.

Social and economic developments

The final decade of the Wars of Religion had caused widespread suffering and hardship amongst the masses. The wars of the 1590s had touched most of France and left a trail of devastation and bloodshed. Peasant suffering was at its most acute in this period, a point reinforced by the frequency and scale of peasant revolt. This period of economic downturn also witnessed a reversal of the social mobility that we witnessed in the first half of the period. Many of those who had made good in the 1520s and perhaps bought titles or lived nobly, now fell back into the third estate. Lesser nobles were hit by spiralling inflation and fixed rents, and were often forced to sell up. The gap between the rich and the poor widened.

QUESTIONS TO CONSIDER

1. How did Henry IV set about restoring peace?

2. How far was the Edict of Nantes based upon the principle of religious unity?

3. To what extent was the depression in the second half of the sixteenth century cased by the Wars of Religion?

CHAPTER 9

The reign of Henry IV, 1594–1610

HOW FAR WAS THE REIGN OF HENRY IV A TURNING POINT IN THE DEVELOPMENT OF THE FRENCH MONARCHY?

The reign of Henry IV has traditionally been viewed as one of inevitable recovery after the chaos of civil conflict. The political and financial recovery overseen by Henry IV was, in the eyes of Edmund Burke writing in the 1790s, an almost automatic process as France moved seamlessly towards Bourbon absolutism in the seventeenth century. More recent scholarship by Jean Pierre Babelon (1982) and Mark Greengrass in *France in the Age of Henri IV* (Longman, 1987) has demonstrated that Henry IV had to '*consciously create the stability of his rule after the wars*' (Greengrass). The assassination of Henry IV in 1610 (see page 141) clouded the judgement of successive commentators and historians, argues Greengrass, who portrayed the reign of Henry as a golden age in which royal authority was enhanced and the nobility put back in their place.

Henry became something to everyone in the seventeenth and eighteenth centuries: to Catholics he was the pious king who restored unity, to monarchists he was the ideal example of good kingship, and to Parisians he was the king who was interested in social welfare and enlightened toleration. Yet Greengrass has endeavoured to portray a more realistic assessment of Henry IV that shows the extent to which the lines of authority were indeed redrawn in this period. Mack Holt reinforces the line taken by Greengrass that Henry IV consciously worked at the restoration of royal authority. His pragmatic policies of appeasement of leaguer nobles and his ultimate aim of unity in religion are highlighted by Holt as evidence of this proactive approach. Similarly, while Greengrass acknowledges that in some senses Henry IV was fortunate to be ruling over a France tired of war and in a period of general economic recovery, the policies of Henry and Sully (see page 138) were nonetheless shrewd and carefully planned.

However, much research has also been carried out by Janine Garrison (*Royaume, Renaissance et Réforme, 1483–1559*, Paris, 1991), Jean Pierre Babelon (*La Renaissance*, 1976) and Emmanuel Le Roy Ladurie (*L'état royal de Louis XI et á Henri IV*, Paris, 1987) to demonstrate that problems still existed with regard to unification and centralisation by the time of Henry's assassination in 1610. A Huguenot minority still existed and fiscal pressures remained harsh on the third estate. Henry IV did not carry out an expansionist foreign policy necessarily through compassion for the plight of his subjects. Indeed, as Greengrass points out, the fact that he mobilised troops three times between 1600 and 1610 suggests that given more time Henry would have committed France to a costly and probably disastrous foreign war against Spain. The Saluzzo question that was left over from Vervins, caused future conflict, as did the Huguenot question left over from Nantes.

Thus, recent work has done much to penetrate the myth of Henry IV as the outright saviour of France and the ruler who laid the foundations for absolutism. The reign was not without problems and strife but, viewed in comparison to what preceded it and viewed in the context of what succeeded it, it becomes convenient to see Henry IV's reign as the turning point in monarchical fortunes.

TO WHAT EXTENT WAS HENRY IV A MODERN KING?

The reign of Henry IV is often seen as a watershed in the history of early modern France. After almost four decades of civil strife, the first Bourbon king re-established the authority of the crown and brought peace and stability to a kingdom ravaged by war. Henry did much to continue the work carried out by his Valois predecessors Louis XII, Francis I and Henry II in terms of good government and the creation of a nation-state. In particular, Henry is credited with the rebuilding of France after the Wars of Religion through:

- centralisation of government and overriding of provincial powers
- payment of debt and restoration of royal finances
- control of the nobility
- legitimate male heirs
- and a successful invasion of Savoy.

Yet, we must be aware of limitations to this argument. Financial constraints prevented Henry making a lasting impression on the European stage and, as always, there were obstacles preventing the effective centralisation of government. Moreover, we might consider Henry fortunate in the context of his reign because most of France was war-weary and ready to work towards a lasting peace. For once, confessional antagonism took second place to more pragmatic concerns, and it is worth considering just how many of Henry IV's reforms were innovative.

WHY WAS THE YEAR 1598 SO IMPORTANT IN THE REIGN OF HENRY IV?

The year 1598 is a crucially important one in the reign of Henry IV: the Edict of Nantes and the Peace of Vervins were both signed in the spring, bringing France's long period of war to a close.

1. The Edict of Nantes

The Edict of Nantes was a compromise peace settlement based loosely on the principle of long-term unity and Gallicanism. Nevertheless, the concessions contained within the royal brevets had the effect of creating a Huguenot state within a state in the Midi region, and to many the Huguenots were a privileged group dependent upon royal favour and finance. Moreover, an edict alone was no guarantee of peace on the ground, as Catherine de Medici had found out. In reality, the Edict of Nantes was little different from the treaties of the previous decades in that Huguenot toleration was still permitted in certain places and surety towns were assured. Henry was fortunate in one respect because, despite the lenient terms of toleration contained within the royal brevets, France was tired of war and ready to embrace peace. This context allowed Henry to take a precarious middle line, appeasing both confessional groups.

Yet we must never lose sight of what really sold the treaty to the Catholic majority: the long-term aim of unity. Huguenot privileges were supposed to be temporary. The edict was certainly not innovative in that it laid out and met the same obstacles which previous settlements had encountered. The edict met stiff opposition from the *parlements* resentful of the creation of Huguenot surety towns and *chambres mi parties*. It took two years of forceful persuasion from Henry himself to persuade the *parlements* to register the edict and even then Rouen avoided formal registration until 1609.

Furthermore, law and order had largely broken down in the localities, particularly in the south-west where local nobles and office holders had become a law unto themselves, raising taxation at will and charging massive interest rates on loans. It took several years to eradicate such brigandage. Finally, Huguenot surety towns and assemblies effectively undermined royal authority and caused general friction. It was no surprise that by 1610 the Huguenots were once more thinking about war.

Henry IV should be given great credit for his twin policies of appeasement and unity which combined to produce a lasting peace settlement. Yet to argue that this peace was popular or innovative would be wrong. Henry certainly benefited from the general feeling of exhaustion that most Frenchmen felt in 1598.

2. The Peace of Vervins

In 1595, having placated most of the great leaguer nobles, Henry felt strong enough to declare war on Spain. Again, given years of civil war this was a shrewd move because it served to unite the country in a national campaign against Philip II and further undermine an important ally of the League. An immediate victory at Fontaine-Française in

June 1595 boosted Henry's status and prestige. The following year, Amiens fell to the French and, when Mercouer, the last Leaguer noble holding out in Brittany, turned over to the new King, Philip II was ready to negotiate peace terms. Nearing death and in financial crisis, Philip was ready to make peace on the terms of 1559.

The Peace of Vervins was signed on 2 May 1598 and accordingly it stated that all towns captured by either side since Cateau-Cambrésis in 1559 should be returned. The treaty therefore returned Calais, Toul, Metz, Verdun and Amiens to France which importantly maintained France's north-eastern frontier. In return, France agreed to papal arbitration over French claims to Saluzzo (seized by the Duke of Savoy in 1588), a responsibility which Clement VIII ignored. In 1600, Henry declared war on Savoy over the Saluzzo question. The resultant peace treaty of 1601 saw Henry give up claims to Saluzzo but receive Bresse, Bugey, Valromey and Gex. Therefore, Vervins as with Nantes, sowed seeds of discontent for the future and peace with Spain was always fragile. Again, Henry was limited by financial constraints and for the most part satisfied himself with funding the Dutch rebels in their fight for independence against Spain and encouraging the Turks to attack Calabria and Naples. Spain similarly looked to cause trouble for Henry, supporting discontented French nobles such as Biron and Bouillon. Trade wars were also commonplace and had it not been for financial constraints Henry might have been more aggressive in his relations with Spain, a point reinforced by the fact that the French King mobilised three times between 1600 and 1610.

Therefore, the portrayal of a frugal, careful and pragmatic king who did not sap the royal coffers with unnecessary foreign adventures needs some readjustment. Initially, Henry sought peace because he had to, but in the long term there seems little doubt that Henry intended a more bellicose foreign policy.

HOW SUCCESSFUL WAS HENRY'S FINANCIAL POLICY?

One of the great achievements of Henry IV was the restoration of royal finances. In 1598, the royal debt stood at 300 million livres while no uniform system of tax collection or assessment existed. By 1608, over half the debt was paid, mortgages on crown property had been redeemed and a large revenue had been accumulated in the treasury. Moreover, central administration had permeated the localities in a more systematic manner than before, and **tax farming** was better regulated.

What was the role of Sully?

The man who deserves to take much of the credit for Henry's financial recovery is **Maximilien de Béthune, Duke of Sully**. Sully was unquestionably the most important minister on the royal council. Many on the council such as Bellièvre (chancellor 1599–1607), Villeroy (foreign affairs) and Brulart de Sillery (chancellor after 1607) were noble, conservative and cautious. Most were veterans of Henry III's reign. Sully on the other hand was Huguenot, adventurous, dynamic and more closely aligned with the King. Sully was diligent, conscientious and energetic as can be seen by the number of areas in which he was involved. Apart from finance, Sully was responsible for royal fortifications, buildings, the navy and artillery and for the general upkeep of highways, bridges and canals.

How was the royal debt liquidised?

Yet by far his most remarkable achievement was to accumulate a reserve of 15 million livres by 1610. The immediate problem facing Sully in 1598 was the royal debt, and the large amounts of money owed to England, the Swiss cantons and individual lenders throughout France. Sully's aim was to reduce the figure bit-by-bit in order gradually to restore the king's credit rating and secure loans once again from the major bankers. Much of the debt was simply written off or renegotiated as France had declared bankruptcy after the Wars of Religion.

- States such as the Swiss cantons were ready to accept immediate token cash repayments which France could afford, rather than wait for total repayment over a long period of time. In the end, the Swiss cantons received only one-seventh of the 36 million livres owed to them.

- Debts with Tuscany were repaid through Henry IV's marriage to Marie de Medici in 1600, whereby 2 million livres were wiped out as part of her dowry by the Grand Duke, Ferdinand I.
- France also owed over 4 million livres to England and only when Elizabeth threatened trade restrictions did Henry agree to pay back some of the debts incurred during the Wars of Religion. Even then, Sully persuaded the English Queen to allow one-third of France's subsidy to the Dutch rebels to count towards its debt repayments, thus continuing Henry's cold war against the Spanish while paying off foreign debts.
- Internal debts and those owed to lesser German princes were often simply ignored and remained unpaid, which provoked resentment and anger but little open hostility.

Sully was not popular during the reign of Henry IV but he was effective in liquidating the past and wiping out the bulk of Henry's debt in a short time. Despite such activity, one-sixteenth of the king's income was still devoted to paying for the Wars of Religion in 1608.

How effective was indirect taxation?

One of the principal features of Sully's ministry was a shift towards indirect taxation. The total levy from the *taille* decreased from 18 million livres to an average of 15.8 million livres between 1600 and 1610. Therefore, the burden on the third estate, which had been so heavy during the Wars of Religion, was relieved slightly and Sully instead concentrated on increasing revenue via indirect taxation. In particular, the main indirect tax was the *gabelle*, levied on a variable basis in five out of six areas of France. The problem here was that it was unequal in its distribution and assessment and in the areas in which the *gabelle* was high people found themselves burdened by increases in the price of salt. The yield from indirect taxes on the whole, however, reflected a strengthened economy after 1600. More efficient collection seemed to be the key although it is worth remembering that, despite the apparent emphasis on indirect taxation, revenue from this source only amounted to around 17 per cent of the total paid into the treasury.

Why was the Pancarte a failure?

Moreover, an innovative indirect tax known as the *pancarte* which constituted a 5 per cent sales tax on all goods for sale at markets in walled towns proved so unpopular that rioting broke out in Poitiers and Angiers in 1601 and again at Limoges the following year. The *pancarte* was abolished in November 1602, thus illustrating the problems in attempting to raise revenue by encroaching upon the privileges of the towns. In reality, while tradition may see Henry IV as a king who genuinely cared about the welfare of his subjects the burden of direct taxation remained heavy and in the *pays d'élections* it contributed an average 49.6 per cent of total revenues (1600–4). Perhaps more importantly Sully was willing to write off unrealistic arrears of tax and at the same time investigate cases of corruption in the local administration of the *taille* and to reapportion the burden around the villages. The breakdown in royal authority during the Wars of Religion had exacerbated the problem of decentralised government and Sully did much to itemise and outlaw abuses in the *taille*.

How did the crown attempt to deal with tax farming?

Sully also tackled the age-old problem of tax farming, described by one contemporary observer as the great destroyer of the kingdom's revenue. Specially constituted commissions of judicial enquiry were established, called *chambres de justice*. Such courts of enquiry did not essentially outlaw or prohibit tax farming, but rather regulated the practice and ensured loyalty and accountability from the officials concerned. Indeed, a properly audited and regulated system of tax farming had its benefits for the crown. Tax farmers were those individuals who collected taxes in the localities. Usually, individual contracts were made with the tax farmers and bids for tax farms went to the highest bidder at auction. The crown would issue the subsequent contract. The problem with the system was that it had been much abused by greedy nobles who took advantage of the semi-anarchy during the Wars of Religion to levy exorbitant rates of taxation and make enormous profits for themselves at the expense of the crown.

As well as investigating corruption, the *chambres de justice* raised money because many officials preferred offering non-refundable loans to the crown rather than face potential ruin at trial. Increased centralisation led to more effective tax collection, and Sully was aided by a general economic recovery throughout Europe after the recession of the 1580s and 1590s. Nevertheless, uniformity in tax collection remained out of the question given the popularity and power of the provincial estates (or *pays d'états*). The *pay d'états* were those provinces such as Brittany and Languedoc in which taxation was levied by the local estates as opposed to the *pays d'élections* where taxation was levied by officials on orders from the king's council. Henry and Sully attempted to unify the means of tax assessment and collection by eroding the privileges of the *pays d'états* and they partly succeeded in Guyenne where eight elections were established to administer the *taille* on behalf of the crown.

However, bitter opposition from the other provincial estates meant the reforms were not applied to the whole kingdom. Provincial estates in Dauphiné, Provence, Languedoc and Burgundy were unwilling to pass tax collection over to royal officials and they were often supported by local nobles in their defence of parochial privilege. Henry risked open revolt by encroaching upon their liberties, but such concessions undermined Henry's authority and both he and Sully regarded the provincial estates as enemies of the crown.

How successful was the Paulette?

One lucrative measure which Sully introduced in 1604 was the *paulette*, a device which allowed royal officials to ensure that their heirs would continue to possess their offices, in return for one-sixtieth of the capital value. Knecht likens the *paulette* to an insurance premium payable by office holders to exempt them from the 40-day rule, while Greengrass sees the strength of the heredity tax lying in its equal appeal to all parties. Certainly, to the office holders it made financial sense as the annual rate was a reasonable payment in return for the continued benefit of their investment by their heirs. For the king the *paulette* created a predictable income from royal offices and removed offices from the patronage of leading nobles. Every office holder who paid the annual sum was reminded that he owed loyalty to the king and the long-term political consequences of the *paulette* should not be underestimated. Venality and the sale of royal offices had long been an important source of revenue for the monarchy but such procedures had not always been advantageous to the authority of the crown. Now the *paulette* ensured that venality took place on the crown's terms and the bribery and corruption involved in the process was officialised and directed into the royal coffers rather than the pockets of influential intermediaries.

ASSESSMENT OF FINANCIAL REFORM

- Under Sully the royal budget achieved a surplus by 1610, standing at 15 million livres.

- Foreign debts were effectively liquidated through advantageous renegotiation or, in the case of Tuscany, marriage.

- Sully maintained a tight control on expenditure and kept a strict budget for artillery, roads and bridges. The court was not lavish and Marie de Medici's expenditure was closely monitored.

- Centralisation improved the collection of taxation and, while corruption and privilege were not eradicated, they were turned to the advantage of the crown, for example by the paulette and the *chambres de justice*.

- Obstacles to the effective administration of the *taille* were insurmountable and the provincial estates remained virtually autonomous in tax collection.

TO WHAT EXTENT WAS HENRY ABLE TO CENTRALISE GOVERNMENT?

The provincial estates and the towns jealously guarded their liberties and privileges with regard to tax exemptions and local government. Henry was eager to extend royal influence into the localities, both to strengthen his own position and to increase revenue. Already Louis XII and to a greater extent Francis I had begun this process of centralisation with varying degrees of success. Certainly royal commissioners in the localities (or *maîtres des requêtes de l'hôtel*) were regularly dispatched to ensure that royal proclamations were upheld and adhered to. Such men were drawn from the court and were not the beneficiaries of venality, therefore they owed total loyalty to the crown.

Under Sully provincial problems were dealt with more effectively by royal commissioners but there were not enough of them and their role was as yet ill-defined. As Knecht observes, the *intendants de justice* became the pillar of royal absolutism under Louis XIII and Louis XIV yet under Sully they were used haphazardly and the traditional obstacles to royal authority still existed, namely the *parlements*, provincial estates, the towns and the nobility. After 40 years of near anarchy, Henry and Sully did a remarkable job in restoring royal authority and the prestige of the crown, and the restoration of royal finances is testament to the extent to which they were able to penetrate parochial barriers. However, despite the widening powers of the *maîtres des requêtes de l'hôtel* and the planting of royal lieutenants in town governments, the centralisation of royal administration still had a long way to go before the king's word immediately became law throughout the kingdom.

TO WHAT EXTENT WAS HENRY ABLE TO CONTROL THE NOBILITY?

Until the birth of Louis in 1601 (who would become Louis XIII) and his brother Gaston in 1608, the Bourbon succession remained uncertain, and therefore aristocratic intrigue continued to remain close to the surface. The legitimacy of **Henry IV's divorce** and subsequent marriage to Marie de Medici was controversial and the blood relationship between Henry and his Valois predecessor so distant that many princes believed their claim to the throne was better. This, combined with Habsburg determination

KEY EVENTS

Henry IV's divorce After Henry's escape from Paris in 1576, Marguerite was finally granted permission to return to her husband in Navarre, and for three and a half years Queen Marguerite and her husband lived a scandalous life in Pau. Both openly kept other lovers, and they quarrelled frequently. Queen Marguerite returned to her brother's court in France after an illness in 1582 but Henry III was soon scandalised by her reputation and forced her to leave the court. After long negotiations, she was allowed to return to her husband's court in Navarre, but she received an icy reception. Determined to overcome her difficulties, Queen Marguerite masterminded a coup d'état and seized power over Agen. After several months of fortifying the city, the citizens of Agen revolted and Queen Marguerite fled to the castle of Carlat. In 1586, she was imprisoned by her brother Henry III in the castle of Usson, in Auvergne, where she spent eighteen years. In 1589, her husband succeeded to the French throne as *Henry IV*. Negotiations to dissolve the marriage were entered in 1592 and concluded in 1599 with an agreement that allowed her to maintain the title of queen. The film, *La Reine Margot* (1993), starring Isabelle Adjani and Daniel Auteuil charts the tempestuous relationship between Henry and Marguerite.

to undermine the Bourbon monarch, contributed to sporadic instability and some noble discontent.

Actually, Henry IV did much to repair the damage of 40 years of civil war through generous pensions, careful regulation of provincial governors and limited numbers of new peers. Inevitably there were those who resented the huge pensions handed out to Leaguer nobles in order to ensure loyalty, and those omitted from the royal council felt ostracised and isolated. Nevertheless, Henry did much to increase the authority of the crown in the localities through the erosion of duties expected of the provincial governors. The governors were encouraged to reside at court, thus giving them the impression that they were sharing in the decision-making process, while more trustworthy lesser nobles were utilised as provincial lieutenants to ensure that the king's will was carried out in the provinces. Such lieutenants limited the seriousness and extent of noble discontent in the localities although two significant noble revolts occurred around Gascony.

How serious were the rebellions of Biron and Bouillon?

In January 1601, Marshal de Biron, who had become an admiral in 1592, marshal in 1594 and provincial governor of Burgundy in 1596 admitted to conspiring with Spanish agents. Despite such treasonable activity, Henry pardoned Biron in the hope that such leniency would be reciprocated with loyalty. Yet Biron was ambitious and very much pro-Spain. After the conflict with Savoy, Biron was once more found to be organising a rebellion to depose Henry IV: in July 1602 he was arrested and then executed in the Bastille. Other nobles in Auvergne and Gascony were implicated and Sully made them beg for forgiveness.

One leading nobleman deeply implicated with Biron and Philip III was the Duke of Bouillon. Like Biron, Bouillon had been close to Henry as a lieutenant-general during the Wars of Religion and he held vast lands in the south-west as well as the principality of Sedan on the German border. Given the fact that Henry IV still owed large amounts of money to German Protestant princes, which had not been forthcoming, Bouillon represented a dangerous focal point for rebellion. Moreover, Bouillon's brother-in-law was

Frederick IV of the Palatinate. Bouillon fled to Sedan and attempted to raise support with Spanish money. Few in France or Geneva rallied to his unconvincing Protestant martyr act, and by 1606 Henry IV had become fed up with continued speculation of an aristocratic conspiracy involving former leaguers and Protestant princes. Henry IV travelled in person to Sedan at the head of a large force. Over 1,000 nobles came before the King on his travels to profess their loyalty and, as Henry prepared to besiege Sedan, Bouillon surrendered in return for a pardon and confirmation of all of his offices.

How did Henry IV maintain loyalty and control against the nobility?

Ultimately, both revolts were overly ambitious and never likely to succeed. Henry dealt effectively with them, preferring by and large to show clemency rather than ruthlessness. Loyalty and control were the keys to Henry's relationship with the nobility and he remained rightfully suspicious of leading noble families such as Condé, Soissons and Guise. Henry could not afford to alienate the princes of the blood and exclude them from power although he did not wish to hand such individuals too much authority. Henry looked to organise marriage alliances among the nobility which maintained old rivalries and kept the grandees disunited in the face of increasing royal authority.

Moreover, Henry was increasingly able to call upon a new group of nobles, the so-called nobility of the robe, who had steadily increased their status and power since 1500. This new administrative noble class had risen through the ranks of office holders and had benefited from the increase in venality. The need for ready cash during the civil wars meant a rapid rise in venality and the number of royal office holders doubled in provinces such as Rouen. The effects were threefold – unsuitable candidates bought positions of power and often profited greatly from them, the associated bureaucracy increased as did the wage bill footed by the crown, and the old nobility of the sword felt threatened by the advance of this new class of noble.

On the other hand, the sale of offices provided a lucrative source of income and the introduction of the *paulette* from

1604 ensured that the crown received an annual income from office holders and maintained some control over them. Moreover, few that bought offices held any great power and to argue that the nobility of the robe challenged the social status of the nobility of the sword would be wrong although some families from new and old did intermarry. The King became increasingly reliant on a trusty inner council to make and break policy – men such as Bellièvre, Villeroy and Sully. The great nobles were not excluded entirely from the decision-making process and certainly they were influential at court. Moreover, it was still the higher nobility that the King relied upon to raise arms and provide loans and Henry dare not antagonise them unnecessarily. Similarly, the nobility depended upon the king for status, power and position and largely it was in their interests to be close to the king. While discontented factions existed within the old nobility, none were united or strong enough to threaten the crown.

WHAT WAS THE IMPACT OF HENRY IV'S ASSASSINATION?

More than twenty attempts were made on Henry's life over the course of his reign, mainly by Catholic extremists who doubted the sincerity of his conversion from Protestantism to Catholicism. Henry's foreign alliances with the Dutch republic, England and the German princes convinced zealous Catholics that he was merely a lapsed heretic. On 14 May 1610, the King travelled from the Louvre to the Arsenal by coach. As the coach stopped in traffic on the rue la Ferronnière, Henry was stabbed three times through the open carriage window. Henry died almost at once while his assassin, Ravaillac, seemingly acting alone, was brutally tortured and then had his body pulled apart by horses.

Some argue that Henry's assassination saved France from a ruinous and disastrous war against Spain while others believe that Henry just planned to give the Habsburgs a sharp lesson in Germany before pursuing his desire to marry his son to the Infanta of Spain. Henry's sudden demise obscures his designs, although his assassination did reveal the dangers of what many construed as an anti-Catholic foreign policy because the assassin, Ravaillac, appears to have acted out of Catholic zeal, certain that Henry was an enemy of the Pope and the true faith.

CONCLUSION: WAS HENRY IV A MODERN KING?

Henry IV, the first Bourbon king, takes his place in French history as the monarch who arrested the decline which France had experienced since 1562. In the process he showed great concern for the welfare of his subjects and restored political and social order to the kingdom. Above all else he put the monarchy on a firm footing economically and enhanced the authority of the crown, paving the way for the absolutism of Louis XIII and Louis XIV. There is little doubt that Henry achieved a great deal in a short period of time, although his reputation was heightened by the fact that he became a royal martyr at the hands of Ravaillac and through the vastly inflated picture of him offered in Sully's memoirs written in 1611 and entitled *Sage et royales économies d'état … de Henri le grand.*

The extent to which Henry cared for the welfare of his subjects is debatable. Certainly the two peace edicts of 1598 were crucially important in giving France some breathing space after 40 years of civil conflict. The Wars of the League in the 1580s and 1590s had been particularly ruinous and, with the economy in tatters and the third estate in revolt in the south-west, Henry recognised the need for peace. Both the Edict of Nantes and the Peace of Vervins were successful in the short term and served their purpose.

The Edict of Nantes remained effective on paper for 87 years although tension was never far from the surface as can be seen in Louis XIII's assault on Protestant Béarn and the subsequent decision by the Reformed assembly at La Rochelle to divide France into eight circles. The Edict of Nantes did not end the Wars of Religion; it was the Peace of Alais in 1629 which fulfilled that role, although it was not until 1685 that the Edict of Nantes was revoked by Louis XIV in a bid to restore unity in France. Similarly, the Peace of Vervins sowed seeds of future discontent with regard to the marquisate of Saluzzo. Henry was bellicose by nature but recognised the need to buy time in order to restore royal finances. Yet his increasing aggression towards the end of his reign revealed his true intentions, and had he not been assassinated it is likely that he would have committed France to all-out war against Spain. Therefore, two important points must be made:

- The Edict of Nantes succeeded in maintaining peace because the population was ready to accept anything which offered a respite in the hostilities. In the long term, the problem of a Huguenot minority in the south still existed.
- Henry did not commit himself to an aggressive foreign policy until 1600 because he did not have the financial resources to do so, not because he did not want to. To argue that he had the welfare of his subjects at heart may be wide of the mark. Had he not been assassinated Henry may have been remembered as the king who took France into a ruinous and disastrous war against Spain.

Unquestionably the finest achievement of Henry's short reign was the restoration of royal finances. Thanks in large part to Sully there was a budgetary surplus of 15 million livres by the end of Henry's reign. A shift towards indirect taxation, a liquidisation of past debts and innovative reforms limiting corruption, all contributed to a steady financial base. Yet, while it was relatively straightforward to liquidate the past and write off old debts the actual economic rebuilding of France at grassroots level was a much more arduous and long-term task. In eastern France, local trade and agricultural had been heavily affected by the Wars of Religion and then Henry's preparations for the siege of Sedan. It was well into the seventeenth century before the industry and population of France saw recovery from the combined ravages of plague, war and famine which had so blighted the kingdom between 1562 and 1598. Moreover, the budgetary surplus of 15 million livres should be compared to the 10 million livres spent by the regent, Marie de Medici, between 1610 and 1614 on magnates such as Condé, Mayenne, Conti and Nevers in order to preserve peace. The purse-strings were certainly loosened after Henry's death and Sully's retirement.

In short:

- Direct taxation remained high in several parts of the kingdom and economic recovery on the ground was slow. The people were still suffering the effects of war after Henry's death.
- The duration of Henry's reign was so short that we cannot expect too much in terms of long-term recovery. The simple recovery of royal finances was a remarkable achievement.

In terms of restoring royal authority and eroding provincial liberties Henry had mixed success. There can be little doubt that Henry did much to raise the prestige and status of the monarchy and he should be praised for the way in which he appeased Leaguer nobles in the 1590s and unified the country in a war against Spain in 1595. Moreover, both the Edict of Nantes and the Peace of Vervins came at the right time and Henry skilfully played a middle line between Huguenot toleration and Catholic desires for unity which ultimately led to further conflict but which brought a sustained period of peace. Few unified aristocratic revolts occurred during Henry's reign, although the disloyal activities of Biron and Bouillon were a sign of things to come.

Both for political and financial purposes Henry tried hard to penetrate local privileges and traditions. Tax farmers were regulated while the *paulette* served to bring in a predictable annual income and ensure loyalty from office holders. Royal lieutenants and *chambres de justice* were not really innovative ideas but in the context of the previous 40 years of warfare it was important that Henry set about re-enforcing the royal will in the countryside and in the towns.

Again, given the duration of his reign could we really expect Henry to break down barriers that had existed for centuries? Provincial estates and urban councils remained thorns in the side of the monarchy and to an extent continued to undermine the authority of the crown. Henry wanted to tax the *pays d'états* more heavily, and through the creation of eight elections in Guyenne he did start to erode their privileges. However, Henry and Sully were never able to impose uniformity of tax collection on the kingdom and probably they never believed it possible. They were trying to restore royal authority and collect as much income as they could from the provinces. It seems clear that the brigandage and abuses carried out by lesser nobles during the Wars of Religion were much less serious during Henry's reign, and the King's idea to encourage royal governors to reside at court set a precedent for future kings. Therefore with regard to centralisation, Henry was able to:

- regulate corruption and increase the yield collected from the *taille*
- and permeate the localities with royal agents who maintained law and order while enforcing the king's will.

However,

- Provincial estates and town councils still held much autonomous power and guarded their privileges fiercely.
- Too few royal commissioners existed to make a significant difference on the ground.

In conclusion, Henry's reputation has probably been inflated over time and in some respects he was fortunate that the people of France were ready for peace at any cost. Moreover, Henry was ably assisted by the very hard-working Sully to whom much credit should be directed. Henry may have been concerned for the welfare of his subjects and the general decrease in direct taxation must have been welcomed. Nevertheless, for the majority of the population, life was still uncertain and hard. Henry himself was primarily interested in restoring the finances and maintaining order – the welfare of his subjects was a by-product rather than a priority. Henry restored royal authority, but such was the nature of French politics it was destined to be short-lived. On his death, Henry left a 9-year-old son to succeed him, namely Louis XIII. The regent was Henry's widow Marie de Medici, ruling with a council dominated by Catholics many of whom were ex-Leaguers. The situation mirrored that of 1559 and the fragility of Henry IV's years of stability was clear for all to see.

CHAPTER SUMMARY: HENRY IV AND SULLY

Here are some key points to remember on Henry IV and Sully:

- Henry IV's reign is traditionally seen as a period of monarchical recovery after the chaos and instability of the Wars of Religion. His abjuration and conversion to Catholicism combined with victory over Spain and cautious appeasement of leaguer nobles ought to be viewed as politically astute moves.
- Henry and his able minister Sully were able to control both tax farming and venality in the interests of the crown through the introduction of the *chambres de justice* and the *paulette*. These were important steps towards re-building monarchical authority. Yet tax farming still existed and whilst the *paulette* ensured a predictable annual income for the crown, it also allowed leading noble families to monopolise particular political offices.
- Sully's great achievement was liquidating the royal debt, which stood at 300 million livres in 1598. Nevertheless as a consequence of his fiscal ruthlessness and increase in indirect taxation (salt, wine and customs) Sully was unpopular with the nobility and merchants. Moreover, one-sixteenth of the king's income was still devoted to paying for the Wars of Religion by 1610.
- Henry's relationship with the nobility demands attention. Clearly his path to coronation had been far from straightforward. The way in which he had bought off the loyalty of Leaguer nobles was effective but had antagonised many who had turned to the crown out of loyalty. There was also disgruntlement from those (both Catholics and Huguenots) who doubted his sincerity in becoming Catholic and who may have been omitted from the royal council. Two significant noble rebellions occurred in Gascony:
  1. 1601 – Marshall Biron
  2. 1606 – Duke of Bouillon
  Both of these rebellions were ambitious and never likely to succeed. Henry remained rightfully wary of leading noble families (Conde, Soissons and Guise) and maintained old rivalries and kept the grandees disunited. Increasing inter-marriage between new and old nobility occurred.

- Henry's reign is often seen as the stepping stone to seventeenth century absolutism in France, but be careful not to overdo this. His reign is relatively short, the nobility and country as a whole were tired of war and financially exhausted and beneath the surface the same issues of provincialism and noble autonomy still existed. Yet like Francis I he was a strong personal monarch, and combined with a period of relative internal stability Henry IV was able to keep a check on the nobles and use them to restore royal authority rather than battle against them. It is no coincidence that Henry looked to the old nobility as a means of re-building the authority of the crown.
- The Edict of Nantes is often seen as the building block of the recovery of France. After all it appeared to succeed where other peace treaties failed. It gave France some breathing space and time to re-build the economy and restore trust and authority in the monarchy. Yet it did not really solve the problem of a Protestant minority in the Midi. If anything the secret brevets endorse their existence. Henry's edict succeeded because the middle ground within France wanted peace at all costs and he was able to win them over. However, its success was in the short-term.

The specification key themes across the period can be summarised as follows:

Nation state
We established that France was not a nation state in 1500, and although there had been some progress in terms of territorial boundaries and linguistic unity, the civil wars had retarded this development significantly. The concept of nationhood was still a foreign one to Frenchmen. Henry IV was more concerned with re-establishing royal authority after years of decay, and in this respect centralisation aided national uniformity and unity.

Relations between the king and his subjects
Taxation demands remained high despite the end of hostilities, as Henry IV and Sully sought to liquidise the royal debt. Peasants in the localities were however, spared the corruption and greed of local *seigneurs* who had taken advantage of the collapse of royal power to exploit the

masses. Like Louis XII at the beginning of the period, Henry IV was perceived to have the interests of the people at heart as he set about restoring the French kingdom to its former glory. Whilst slightly misguided, it is true that the third estate welcomed a period of peace.

Religious developments

Protestantism had been the major divisive factor in this period, and to an extent Henry IV was able to restore religious unity in the Edict of Nantes. At least a settlement was drawn up which convinced Catholics that the long-term goal of unity was attainable. In reality, the Edict of Nantes stored up religious problems for the future. Henry IV was fortunate that most of the population were sick of war and wanted peace at any cost.

Social and economic developments

People were still suffering the economic effects of the Wars of Religion well after Henry's death, but at least the Edict of Nantes heralded a period of relative stability on which economic recovery could begin. The third estate saw no change in their political or economic status during Henry IV's reign and their existence continued to revolve around the village community, the seasons and the land. Henry IV's reign was too short to expect radical social and economic changes, and this was not his agenda anyway. Henry IV brought peace to France, something his Valois predecessors had failed to do and for this he was acclaimed as something of a saviour. In reality, the French economy was aided by a general economic upturn in Europe and some reasonable harvest yields.

QUESTIONS TO CONSIDER

1. How did Henry IV set about restoring peace?

2. How far was the Edict of Nantes based upon the principle of religious unity?

3. To what extent was the depression in the second half of the sixteenth century caused by the Wars of Religion?

SUMMARY

The Development of the Nation State: France 1498–1610

Now that we have been through the period chronologically, let us look at some of the themes in the development of the nation state in more detail.

Why did the power of the monarchy fluctuate 1498–1610?

- Monarchical strength was very much dependent upon the personal character and rule of the individual monarch alongside the political, religious and economic circumstances of the reign, which were often out of his control.
- French monarchy rested upon fundamental principles of divine rule, Catholicism, judicial supremacy and armed force when required. In particular the French monarchy was held to be sacred and when this was undermined in the 1580s so the power of the monarch declined.
- French monarchs were never absolute, not even in the reigns of Francis I and Henry II. Knecht talks of '*limited absolutism*' in that practical limitations on the ground always existed. Louis XII and Francis I introduced centralising agencies but these were undermined by political collapse in the 1580s. Theories of absolutism (Bodin and Bude) existed to further the image of a powerful monarch, but a monarch that overrides all representative institutions and holds power of life and death over each subject verges on tyranny.
- Religion was the key issue that undermined the French monarchy post 1562 and especially in the 1580s. Radical Huguenots advocated resistance after St Bartholomew's Day whilst Leaguers called for regicide during the succession crisis and mismanagement of Henry III. The Wars of Religion put an end to the centralising policies of French monarchs and restored provincial, parochial power in the localities.
- A strong monarchy also requires secure finances, something which was made impossible by war throughout the period. The Italian Wars begun by Louis XII became increasingly expensive up to 1559. The civil

wars were even more damaging because the fighting took place on French soil. By 1580 Henry III simply did not have the resources to defeat the Huguenots. Increasing fiscal pressure also had social implications demonstrated by popular unrest throughout the period.

- The relationship between the sovereign and the nobility remained crucial throughout the period. The reliance upon the old aristocracy continued to be vital in order to maintain law and order and to raise armies. The rise of the nobility of the robe gave the king a new administrative class of noble but did not really diminish the potential threat of rebellion by the nobility of the sword. Venality also allowed offices to become dominated by certain families, offsetting its financial significance. Again, it was religion which divided the nobility and by the 1580s a significant number of both Huguenot and Catholic nobles were against the king.

- Throughout the period, strong kings showed the power to override representative institutions but were never able to abolish them entirely. *Parlement*s still ratified legislation and the Estates General still existed as a potential forum for grievances to be aired. Similarly before taxation was granted in the *pays d'etats,* the monarch had to listen to provincial grievances. The real danger came in the 1580s when institutions such as the League were out of the control of the crown (Nemours) and foreign aid undermined French monarchy.

- French kings appear to have had no master plan for absolutism during this period but merely looked to advance their own power. Centralisation meant more effective control over the localities and more efficient collection of taxes. However, the kings realised that in order to run France effectively a balance had to be maintained on the ground between monarchical rule and local power bases be they noble, urban or rural.

- The recovery of monarchical power by Henry IV was relatively superficial in that the situation of 1610 mirrors that of 1559 with a boy king and a regency government in place. With hindsight it can be argued that Henry IV set France on the road to absolutism but the contemporary perception was different. In reality Henry had little option but to be prudent – again circumstances dictated policy.

- Clearly the fortunes of the monarchy fluctuate throughout this period. The economy, religion, social change and personal character all affected the nature and development of monarchical power in France.

How important were the nobility in the development of France?

- Monarchy gave the nobility status and exemption from tax whilst the nobility in return offered arms and loyalty to the crown. The fact that the nobility of the sword served the king in Italy during the Habsburg-Valois Wars is often cited as one reason why there was little domestic unrest in the first half of the century. However, the constant state of war took its toll on the finances of the nobility.
- Until the mid-sixteenth century threats to the crown from the nobility were rare. However, the Bourbon rebellion of 1523 over land inheritance was dangerous because it involved foreign troops (under Charles V and Henry VIII).
- The death of Henry II and accession of the 15-year-old Francis II in 1559 is the key turning point. The power vacuum allowed noble faction to grow in power (particularly the Guise family). This was further fuelled by religious tension and results in the Conspiracy of Amboise where the Huguenots tried to seize the king.
- The Wars of Religion served to divide the nobility and radicalise their political outlooks. 40 per cent of nobles became Calvinist and offered the movement money and legitimacy as well as offering fellow members of the faith protection on their estates. These Huguenot nobles formed a key group which opposed the policies of the crown and fought for religious toleration. Post 1572 they even opposed the institution of the crown itself. The monarchy recognised the power of the Huguenot nobility because every peace treaty included the rights of Huguenot nobles to worship.
- Those nobles who remained Catholic were spurred into action after the failure of the crown to defeat the Huguenots outright. The death of Anjou in 1584 was a key turning point as fear of a Protestant succession to the thrown grew. This led to the formation and growth of the Catholic League which highlights the radicalisation

of the Catholic nobility. The complete breakdown of the relationship between the Catholic nobles and the king is demonstrated by the Treaty of Nemours in 1585 and the assassination of the Guises in 1588.

- The restoration of law and order in the localities during the reign of Henry IV demonstrates the importance of the nobility to the Crown. Henry's policy of buying off Leaguer nobles and appeasing Huguenots was successful although he too faced noble rebellion from Biron and Bouillon. Another development in the time of Henry IV was the increasing importance of court. In order to attain favour and patronage, nobles during Henry's reign were required to spend most of their time there. This meant that the king could appoint loyal provincial governors, keep a close eye on the nobles at court and drain noble finances (life at court was expensive).

Conclusions:

- The nobility faced many adjustments over the course of the sixteenth century but fundamentally the old nobility retained a central role in the governing of the country and a place towards the top of the social hierarchy.
- There was a steady movement in and out of the nobility (social mobility). Middling farmers or wealthy peasants who benefited from the economic boom at the start of the period might assume noble status by simply living nobly. With the onset of depression they might as easily fall back into the Third Estate.
- Noble status brought with it exemption from royal tax, therefore French kings sought to tighten up the qualifications for noble standing. A noble order was created in 1578 entitled the Order of the Holy Spirit bringing together the most distinguished families. This was also a method of controlling the most powerful noble families.
- The old established noble families maintained their status whilst some of the lesser nobles who had less material and landed wealth struggled, especially during the Wars of Religion.
- It became increasingly important for the nobility to be seen and even reside at court. Such a trend began under the Renaissance monarchy of Francis I when court life

became critical for power and patronage. Pensions, tax farming contracts and offices might be attainable at court whilst proximity to the king brought power. Although not as important as in the seventeenth century, the nobility came to recognise the importance of court.

- The wealthy, landed nobility actually benefited from the depression of the second half of the century just as they had struggled during the recovery of the first half. An overpopulated society, low wages and high agricultural prices suited them well. Wealthy nobles might buy the land of lesser nobles, as the latter struggled to cope with fixed rents in times of inflation.
- A key point therefore is that the wealthier, top echelon of nobility detached itself from the lesser nobility.
- The market for offices increased in France. Venality became systematic and assumed great importance as a source of revenue for the crown. As a result of ennoblement through office, a significant new class, the *noblesse de robe*, emerged to challenge the political power, if not social predominance of the nobility of ancient lineage.
- The councillors of Francis I and Henry II were princes of the royal blood but by the second half of the century, although the high nobility retained its majority in the small inner council (Montmorency, Guise etc), it had lost its dominance over the larger councils which dealt with routine administration. By 1598 the king's council was dominated by the nobility of the robe (with the important exception of Sully).
- The factious behaviour of the upper nobility during the French Wars of Religion perhaps taught Henry IV that they needed to be excluded from administrative positions. Yet the way in which he bought off Leaguer nobles does show that he still needed their support in the provinces. Therefore, provincial governships and military commands remained the preserve of the *noblesse d'épée*.
- The lucrative nature of venality led to more offices being created and further layers of bureaucracy which hampered effective government (there were two chief treasurers in the 1590s). The introduction of the *paulette* suspended the 40 day rule (resignations of office were invalid and subject to forfeiture to the crown unless the

owner survived 40 days after making the act of resignation), on condition that office holders paid an annual tax equivalent to 1/60 of the value of the office.

- Venality and especially the Paulette brought in a predictable income by the 1590s but more than ever offices became dominated by certain families and it was rare for the crown to be able to buy out noble families. In France an office was accepted as a piece of private property which could be bought, sold and transmitted in family settlements, just like a plot of land.
- Over time some *noblesse de robe* would inter marry and assimilate with the *noblesse d'épée* yet in the sixteenth century they were more like a fourth estate.
- Noble rebellion was an ever-present threat to the monarchy if that monarch was weak or if he encroached upon the liberties of the respective noble.
- The power vacuum caused by boy kings (Francis II, Charles IX) and the regency under Catherine provided ambitious noble families such as Guise an opportunity to pursue their own ambitions. This factious behaviour was exacerbated by religious division.

What was life like for the third Estate?

- The standard of living for the Third Estate was often out of their control. The Wars of Religion and the **mini ice age** contribute significantly to the increased poverty of the Third Estate in the second half of the sixteenth century.
- During the sixteenth century the problem of poverty grew worse, and whilst there were some measures of poor relief established they were not very systematic. Lyon established a poor relief scheme which offered tickets of entitlement to poor relief which were issued to the needy poor. Every Sunday morning bread and money were distributed to the needy poor. Poor orphans were taken into children's hospitals. By the mid century, Lyons had instituted a compulsory levy and Paris introduced a poor tax.
- The guiding principles established during the sixteenth century with regards to poor relief would be that it was the moral obligation of the Christian community and a necessary measure to maintain order and control. It was no real surprise that Lyon reformed its poor relief system

after the Grand Rebeyne had severely disturbed the social order there. It is also worth noting that there were few systematic royal measures to meet the growing poverty and suffering within France. The crown remained more interested in exploiting the Third Estate rather than helping it.

- The Third Estate remained fundamentally unrepresented at a political level. Estates General did not meet the demands of the rural peasantry and for the first half of the sixteenth century did not meet at all. *Parlements* and town councils may have defended the interests of the population through a defence of privileges and traditions but did not really represent the interests of the peasantry. Often the only means of making their views heard was through rebellion. Popular rebellion became more common in the second half of the sixteenth century as economic and social conditions worsened.

- Third Estate life revolved around the village and was relatively inward looking. Peasantry were only concerned with high political decisions when it affected them and this was more the case in the 1580s and 1590s when civil war was more widespread in its impact and intense in its effects. Communal bonds were built up around land and the church. Both of these areas come under threat in the second half of the sixteenth century. Pressure on land, inflation and rise in rents, forced some into the cities whilst the rise of Calvinism threatened the existence of a community of believers.

- In periods of economic boom and prosperity the Third Estate benefited through cheaper rents, stable prices and high wages. The price revolution and demographic rise hit farmers hard and led to a small group of wealthy farmers emerging, many of them urban in origin.

- With economic depression we see the rise of the economic day labourer in the sixteenth century. They might have owned a small amount of land, but were dependent upon day labour which was often seasonal. In the second half of the century big landowners paid lower wages due to economic depression and a growing population.

- The urban experience of the Third Estate differed from the rural experience. Plague, disease and employment all differed in the cities. The number and size of cities grew within France throughout the sixteenth century. The Grand Rebeyne is an early example of an urban riot in which grain was seized from warehouses and the houses of wealthy citizens. Cities were potentially more explosive environments because there were large numbers of people in the same place (demonstrated by St Bartholomew's Day). Whereas popular violence in the countryside tended to be aimed at the *seigneurs* and landowners, urban violence centred upon tax collectors or municipal officials. The same principle applies to both; the wealthy wanted to control the poor and ensure that order was upheld.

- The ordinary lives of the Third Estate were hit hardest by the subsistence crisis of the mid-sixteenth century which was in turn exacerbated by the Wars of Religion. This was what affected their lives more than anything, including religion. The religion factor varied from region to region and as St Bartholomew's Day shows was more of an issue where there were communities of two faiths living close together. By the 1580s religious boundaries were more defined and it was the economic depression that was the major concern of the peasants.

What were the economic and social developments in this period?

- Between 8 and 9 out of every 10 persons in France at the beginning of the sixteenth century were members of the peasantry – this did not change across the period.
- Life expectancy amongst the peasantry was around 20 years of age throughout the sixteenth century. Literacy levels were 5–8 per cent and increased slightly over the 100 year period.
- The French population grew rapidly over the course of the sixteenth century but then levelled out towards the end. It grew from 13 to 18 million in the first 50 years but by 1600 was somewhere between 19 and 20 million people.
- Grain prices doubled in the first six decades of the sixteenth century and the cost of agricultural produce in general went up by 35 per cent in the period 1550–1600. By 1600 the average nominal price of grain was five times as high as it had been in 1520.

- By 1559 the royal debt at Lyon amounted to 11.7 million livres and the annual cost of servicing it 2.2 million livres.
- Successive kings at the beginning of the sixteenth century granted protective measures and privileges to various industries (Rouen – textiles, Nimes – draperie, Lyon – silk and Paris – printing).
- However, throughout the period there was little royal input into agricultural reform or stimulation of trade and as a result there was major stagnation in both these areas.
- In 1522 Francis I began the practice of issuing government bonds as rents guaranteed by the Paris *Hotel de Ville* and under Henry II there was a major expansion in this form of credit with the Lyon *Grand Parti*.
- The *taille* rose from 2.4 million livres in 1515 to 4.6 million livres in 1544, but was still inadequate to meet the needs of Francis I.
- All taxes which had totalled 5 million livres in 1523 reached 13 million in 1559.
- In the period 1562–98 during the Wars of Religion, Bordeaux wine exports fell by 30 per cent. Similarly the textiles industry in the north of France was hit hard by the disruption caused by war.
- Sieges such as those experienced by the inhabitants of Rouen from 1590 to 1592 and Paris between 1589 and 1594 took a heavy toll on urban populations.
- Although the general pattern was one of depression in the years 1562–98 a few areas continued to experience economic growth during the Wars of Religion. Nantes and La Rochellle benefited from the shift in trade from the Mediterranean to the Atlantic, whilst Marseilles expanded as a result of Venetian problems with the Turks.
- Before 1584 the impact of the Wars of Religion was intensely localised with some regions suffering more than others. Between 1584–98 the wars affected virtually every area of France.
- France would have suffered a depression with or without the Wars of Religion. The periods 1565–68, 1570–73 and most of the 1590s have been identified as ones of low harvest yields. War exacerbated the depression felt by the people of France.

- The succession of peasant uprisings after 1575 were a direct response to the desperate circumstances brought about by war.
- The *paulette* and income from royal offices yielded an average of 7.2% of total revenue between 1600–04
- Only a minority of peasants (1/5) owned more than 5 hectares (the minimum needed for self sufficiency).

How important was religion in the development of France?

Religion is probably the most important theme over the course of the sixteenth century. Let us first identify areas of change and continuity:

Aspects of change

- Growth of Calvinism throughout the 1540s, 1550s and 60s
- Breakdown of royal authority on the back of religious civil war
- Noble support for Calvinism from 1550s onwards
- Legal recognition of Huguenots 1562–98
- Radical revolutionary resistance theories
- Nature of Catholic activism

Aspects of continuity

- Central concept of unity under one faith remained the guiding light for the majority
- Gallican principles bond together a community of believers
- Majority of Frenchmen remain Catholic
- Catholicism of the crown
- Foreign policy objectives ignored confessional loyalties
- Heresy was linked with rebellion and disorder

Some important points:

- The authority of French monarchs rested upon the sacred nature of their kingship, symbolising the importance of Gallicanism.
- Throughout the period in question, French kings tried to uphold their coronation oath to stamp out heresy.

- The growth of Calvinism significantly undermined the authority of the crown.
- The Day of the Placards confirmed Francis's concerns over heresy rather than initiated a new policy of repression.
- Favourable circumstances along with noble support explain the rise of Calvinism in France, yet 90 per cent of the population remained Catholic.
- Catherine de Medici's policies of conciliation served to undermine the principles upon which the authority of the crown rested.
- The power vacuum at court and noble support for Calvinism compromised Catherine's position and put the regent in an awkward political situation.
- The role of religion in the civil wars was central, shaping peace settlements and providing the guiding principle for the Catholic League at a high political level as well as inciting the massacres of 1572 on a more popular level.
- Religion ought to be viewed in a social rather than doctrinal sense. That is to say that the existence of Calvinism amongst a community of believers struck at the core of Gallicanism and the existence of Huguenot churches and *chambre mi parties* were more painful to Catholics than doctrinal debate.
- Throughout the period, religion is tied to political and economic factors, an issue exacerbated by the Wars of Religion.

EXAM STYLE QUESTIONS

Questions in the exam will be centred around the five main themes. Here are some examples of each.

Monarchy

1. 'Supreme in theory, limited in practice'. How far do you agree with this view of the power of the French monarchy in the period from 1498–1610?
2. How far did Henry IV continue the domestic policies of the previous kings of France from 1498?
3. How far did the reign of Francis I mark a turning point in the development of the French nation state from 1498–1610?
4. How effective was the French monarchy in ruling France in the period 1498–1610?

Subjects

1. How do you account for the changing relations between the French kings and their subjects in the course of the period 1498–1610?
2. Assess the importance of the nobility in the development of the nation state in France in the period 1498–1610.
3. Which subjects benefited **most** from French governments during the period 1498–1610?
4. To what extent did life get harder for the people of France in the period 1498–1610?

Social and economic developments

1. Assess the reasons why economic problems were difficult to solve in France from 1498–1610.
2. Assess the importance of economic change in the development of the French nation state during the period 1498–1610.
3. To what extent was civil war the main reason for the decline of the French economy in the second half of the sixteenth century?
4. 'Boom and bust.' How far does this statement explain the nature of the French economy in the period 1498–1610?

Religion

1. How serious a threat was Protestantism to the internal stability of France during the period 1498–1610?
2. Assess the importance of religion in the development of France as a nation state in the sixteenth century?
3. Explain why civil war was so prominent in France in the second half of the sixteenth century but did not occur in the first half of the century.
4. Assess the impact of Protestantism on the unity of France during the years 1498–1610?

The development of the nation state

1. Assess how far France became a more unified state during the period 1498–1610.
2. To what extent did civil war in France disrupt the emergence of a nation state?
3. 'France was made but Frenchmen were not'. How far do you agree with this statement in relation to the period 1498–1610 in France?
4. To what extent had a nation state emerged in France by 1610?

Exam Café
Relax, refresh, result!

Relax and prepare

Ben

When I first started the A2 course I couldn't believe how much there was to cover! It was not until a few weeks later that I realised that it's different from AS because it's looking for continuity and change across a wide period and therefore huge amounts of detailed knowledge on specific events are not needed.

Sophie

I had a real shock when I did my mock exam for this one. I totally ran out of time and did not get through the whole period. It was only when my teacher explained that you need to organise your answer into themes for each paragraph rather than cover the whole period chronologically that I realised where I had gone wrong.

Student tips

Mal

I found it really helpful to think of the whole period as a line graph with low and highpoints – these points are the turning points of the period and the bits that you need to focus on.

Mannjit

Yes, I found the mock exam a bit of an eye-opener too! I was so worried about running out of time that I didn't plan my essays at all and got into a real mess as I realised that I'd forgotten to include bits as I went on. My teacher then made us practise loads of essay plans when we were revising and it really paid off in the exam!

Here are the key ideas and issues that you need to revise for the five major themes: Monarchy, Economy, experience of French Subjects, Religion, the development of the Nation State

Monarchy

- Limitations of monarchical power throughout this period.
- The importance of the personal character and strength of monarchs.
- The strength of Renaissance kingship under Louis XII, Francis I and Henry II.
- Monarchical weakness caused by the French Wars of Religion (1562–98).
- A recovery of power under Henry IV.

Economy

- The growing fiscal demands of the crown and inequalities within society.
- Social implications of economic change (Third Estate and nobility).
- Reasons for stagnation in the French economy.
- Economic recovery under Sully.

Subjects

- The relationship between crown and subjects (the extent to which the crown ruled in the interests of the people – key issue of who benefited and who lost out).
- Specific changes in the makeup and power of the nobility linked to political/religious/economic issues.
- Specific changes in the life of the Third Estate linked to economic/political and religious change.
- Religious experiences of subjects.

Religion

- Unity provided by Catholicism pre 1562.
- The impact of humanism/Lutheranism leading up to the Day of the Placards (1534).
- The social impact of Calvinism leading up to St Bartholomew's Day (1572).
- The political impact of Calvinism leading up to the assassination of Henry III (1588).
- The economic impact of Calvinism leading up to the Edict of Nantes (1598).
- The issue of Protestantism as a divisive factor within France and the extent to which Henry IV resolves this problem.

Nation State

- The extent to which France developed a sense of nationhood over this one hundred year period.
- A consideration of different indicators of nationhood – territorial boundaries, culture, language, law and religion.
- The major obstacles to nationhood such as provincialism and Protestantism.
- The role of the monarchy in forging a nation state.

A Revision Exercise

The following are all pieces of evidence you might use in an essay on monarchical power. Group them into the different themes on page 148 and then explain their significance in a sentence.

- Ordinance of Blois (1499) and Ordinance of Lyons (1510)
- Concordat of Bologna 1516
- Bourbon Rebellion 1523
- Day of the Placards
- 1539 Rouen *Parlement* closure
- Creation of *Chambre Ardente*
- Death of Henry II 1559
- Conspiracy of Amboise 1560
- Estates General 1560 and 1561
- Edict of January 1562
- St Bartholomew's Day Massacre 1572

- *Six Books of the Commonwealth* by Bodin 1576
- Formation of the Catholic League 1576 and 1584
- Death of Anjou 1584
- Day of the Barricades 1588
- Assassination of Henry III 1589
- Abjuration of Navarre 1593
- Peasant Uprisings in the south west 1593–94
- Edict of Nantes 1598

Get the result!

How to write a synoptic essay

1. It is crucial to spend part of your time in the exam planning your essay. This will help you to form an argument and select evidence which backs it up.

2. Try to structure paragraphs around themes that will then allow you to cover the whole 100 year period in every paragraph rather than the whole essay taking a chronological approach.

3. Try to select your evidence widely from across the period. Be prepared to explain your points briefly but succinctly in order to demonstrate your point.

4. Introductions and conclusions must be complete and clear. Your whole argument needs to be in place and key areas of change and continuity identified in each.

5. Highlight turning points and pick out specific examples.

6. Be very clear in your own mind what the arguments are before the examination and then just mould them to fit the question. Remember that if it is a 'how far' or 'to what extent' question, you need to include a range of factors.

How far was France unified as a nation state by 1610?

Examiner's comments

This introduction begins well by defining what is meant by 'nation state'. Sophie then gives her judgement on the question and backs it up with evidence. If she develops this throughout the essay this will be a good answer!

Sophie's answer

In 1498 France lacked the common borders, language, legal system and centralised government that combine to form the basic outline of a nation state. Whilst some progress was made in the evolution of such a state throughout the sixteenth century there remained serious obstacles to national unity. Most notably, religion served as the central divisive factor in the second half of the sixteenth century with the arrival of Calvinism undermining the one true faith that had previously bound France together as a community of believers. Moreover the impact of the French Wars of Religion in a social and economic context served to further erode political centralisation and swung the balance of power back to a provincial or parochial outlook. Ultimately the concept of a united French nation with a shared national outlook would take some time to develop.

Examiner's comments

This first paragraph deals with the theme of territory. It is encouraging to see that Sophie has started using a thematic approach in each paragraph which covers all of the period.

Given the relatively new acquisition of much territory into the French kingdom it is unsurprising that a nation state failed to emerge over the course of the sixteenth century. In 1500 nearly one fourth of the kingdom had been acquired in the previous fifty years either through marriage, conquest or inheritance. Burgundy, Picardy, and Provence were all provinces that had been absorbed into a French kingdom with only loose territorial boundaries. It would take some time for the inhabitants of newly acquired provinces to think as Frenchmen, as what tied them together as individual communities was more provincially based than it was nationally. Moreover, in becoming part of the French kingdom many of these provinces retained local privileges which ultimately undermined any sense of nationhood. The pays d'etats, for example were provinces which could levy and collect their own taxation. Brittany was a crucial strategic addition to the kingdom in 1532 as now the whole Channel coast was under French rule. Successive marriages to Anne of Brittany by Charles VII and

Louis XII show how important the annexation of Brittany was to the crown. Therefore, the lack of clearly defined boundaries hindered the development of a nation state although the emergence of the modern hexagon did begin in the sixteenth century with the acquisition of territories such as Calais, Metz, Toul and Verdun — the problem would lie with uniting such diverse provinces. Still, the creation of a Huguenot Midi during the Wars of Religion significantly undermines territorial unity.

The central locomotive for change in the area of centralisation and the forging of a nation state was the monarchy. The monarchy provided the infant French kingdom with a common denominator across all areas. It was through the French monarchy that a nation state could be forged, although often the intentions of individual monarchs were a good deal more self-centred than the evolution of a nation state. Clearly a centralised and efficiently bureaucratic state would enhance the power of the crown whilst also bringing together diverse legal systems and political privileges. The creation of new parlements in Bordeaux and Rouen along with the introduction of royal officers in the provinces such as the gens de finances were attempts by the French crown to enhance its authority over the localities. Yet, centralisation does not necessarily equate with nationhood, and there is no evidence that strong personal monarchs engendered a popular sense of belonging to France amongst the people. Moreover, whilst the new parlements may have carried out the king's bidding in times of monarchical strength under rulers such as Francis I, they could also undermine the power of the crown as was seen in the reign of Henry III when the parlement of Paris resisted ratification of peace edicts. In short the monarchy alone was unable to forge a nation state as there were so many other factors out of its control that were crucial. Loyalty to a

Examiner's comments

Sophie effectively argues her case here that early attempts at centralisation did not necessarily move France any closer towards nationhood. Looking at the ongoing obstacles to nationhood and the problems faced by French kings in this period is an important aspect to this essay.

sovereign figurehead is simply not enough to define a nation state and on the whole French monarchs lacked the resources, and at times the will, to erode parochial privileges. The Wars of Religion significantly undermined the status of the crown and any move towards nationhood. In particular the formation of the Catholic League during the succession crisis shows us how French Catholics were willing to look to the King of Spain, Philip II for leadership and money rather than their own monarch – hardly a ringing endorsement of national unity. Similarly the Huguenots called on aid from England and the Palatinate. Foreign armies and nobles on French soil did little to create a sense of national identity.

Examiner's comments

Sophie has organised her ideas effectively in this essay. She does not get bogged down in the narrative of events.

Nevertheless, it could be argued that the foundation of a nation state had been laid. After all Francis I's Edict of Villers-Cotterets (1539) insisted on the use of French in all legal documents, although regional dialects continued to be the popular medium for communication at the end of the period. Legal and academic minds were using French as illustrated by Joachim du Bellay's <u>Defence and Illustration of the French Language</u> (1549) yet there was no systematic attempt to enforce the use of French upon the populace. Similarly whilst some ground was made in codifying the legal system and eroding customary law most notably under Louis XII, it was still evident that by the end of the period, provinces clung on to their own traditions and customs. It was always difficult to erode local privileges as the failed pancarte demonstrates. Furthermore the dispute over whether Salic Law took precedence over the Catholicity of the crown in 1584 demonstrates that there were still ambiguities in how the law could be interpreted. Therefore in the realms of language, law and finance there was only marginal progress towards a nation state and often changes at a high political level were not to have any effect on the ground.

It might be argued that French victories abroad and royal control over the church served to advance the cause of a nation state. Yet French gains in Italy were short lived and often the need to raise war time tax caused more shared pain amongst the Third Estate than glory. However, the reaction of the provincial estates of Burgundy in 1526 to the Treaty of Madrid does give us some insight into the emergence of a collective outlook and similarly in 1595, Henry IV was able to stir up a greater sense on national spirit in driving Spanish troops off French soil. When the threat of foreign invasion was at hand there was more likelihood of a national outlook than when the French crown was trying to conquer distant Italian territories.

It is important to recognise that religion provided the French kingdom with a common spiritual outlook in 1500 and that the status of the monarch depended upon his coronation vow to battle against heresy. By 1610 that community of believers had been undermined by the arrival of Calvinism which provided a clear and visible threat to the social and political order within France. The forging of a nation state was undermined by the Wars of Religion and their impact upon France in the second half of the sixteenth century. Calvinism divided the French nobility, most notably in the 1580s when extreme Catholic nobles joined the League and looked to Spain for aid in maintaining the Catholicity of the crown. Clearly religion and political faction took precedence with Leaguer nobles over national loyalty. Since the 1560s a disproportionately large number of nobles had embraced the Huguenot cause and offered it crucial military and financial aid. The social impact of Calvinism can be seen in the St Bartholomew's Day Massacre where Catholic Parisians did not see Huguenots as Frenchmen nor even as human beings as they were slaughtered in a ritualistic and symbolic manner. Huguenots were seen as seditious rebels undermining every aspect of the kingdom but the survival of the Calvinist cause and the failure of the French monarchy to eradicate heresy had a serious impact upon France. By the 1590s peasants of both faiths were united against seigneurial oppression and exploitation whilst Henry IV was able to utilise the general feeling of war exhaustion to usher in a

Examiner's comments

Again, one can see that analysis takes precedence over narrative.

peace that still offered toleration to Huguenots. A nation state in western Europe at the beginning of the sixteenth century would have undoubtedly revolved around the principle of one faith, but by the end of the period that principle had been shaken to its core. Economic and industrial stagnation, rural discontent, monarchical collapse and financial ruin were all consequences of thirty five years of religious war.

Examiner's comments

Sophie finishes an excellent essay with a well balanced and wide ranging conclusion.

In conclusion, there had been some areas in which France had moved towards the creation of a nation state such as codification of the legal system and acquisition of territory. French monarchs such as Louis XII and Francis I had endeavoured to create a more centralised and bureaucratic form of government that went some way towards uniting French provinces under the authority of the crown. Yet provincialism still prevailed and parochial outlooks still held sway over national ones. During the Wars of Religion power lay firmly in the localities as noble exploitation and tax farming would suggest. Henry IV and Sully did much in a short space of time to restore peace and a sense of national identity. Yet it was only the foundations of real change that had been laid. Change often induced opposition and the second half of the sixteenth century weakened the capacity of French kings to introduce reform. A nation state and the sense of a shared culture would emerge slowly over the course of the late seventeenth and eighteenth centuries, rather than quickly out of the relative chaos of the sixteenth century.

BIBLIOGRAPHY

P. Benedict, *Rouen during the Wars of Religion*, Cambridge, 1981

R. Briggs, *Early Modern France 1560–1715*, Oxford, 1977

B. B. Diefendorf, *Beneath the Cross: Catholics and Huguenots in Sixteenth Century Paris*, Oxford, 1991

M. Greengrass, *France in the Age of Henri IV*, London, 1984

M. Greengrass, *The French Reformation*, London, 1987

M. P. Holt, *The French Wars of Religion, 1562–1629*, Cambridge, 1995

M. P. Holt (ed.), *Renaissance and Reformation France*, Oxford, 2002

R. J. Knecht, *French Renaissance Monarchy: Francis I and Henry II*, London, 1996

R. J. Knecht, *The Rise and Fall of Renaissance France 1483–1610*, Oxford, 2001

R. J. Knecht, *Renaissance Warrior and Patron: The Reign of Francis I*, Cambridge, 1994

J. Russel Major, *Representative Government in Early Modern France*, New Haven, 1980

D.H. Pennington, *Europe in the Seventeenth Century*, London, 1989

D. Potter, *A History of France, 1460–1560: The Emergence of a Nation State*, London, 1995

N. Zemon Davis, *Society and Culture in Early Modern France*, Stanford, 1975

GLOSSARY

The Assembly of Notables A group of clergy, nobles and royal office holders personally selected and summoned by the king to consult on national affairs.

Bailli A local royal official whose job it was to ensure that the royal decree was carried out in that area (*bailliage*).

Brevet Clauses within a treaty which were enacted by the monarch without ratification by *parlement*.

Cahier de doléances Complaints presented to the king by each estate at a meeting of the Estates General.

Concordat A concordat is an agreement made between Church and state.

Conseil des affaires The inner cabinet of the king's council made up of his most trusted advisers. It was here that major policy decisions were taken.

Croquants Peasants were dubbed *croquants* (meaning country bumpkins) by their socially superior opponents.

The Estates General A national representative body made up of elected representatives from the clergy, nobility and third estate. Called by the king, usually to discuss and debate matters of critical importance.

Evangelicals Those who believe in the authority of scripture. In the sixteenth century, they advocated reform based on the word of God. Generally, evangelicals were more moderate than Protestants.

Gabelle A tax levied on salt in five areas out of six within France.

Huguenots French Calvinists

Iconoclasts More extreme Protestants believed that the Catholic Church was ruled by the Devil and that religious decorations contravened the commandment against idolatry. The destruction of such images is called iconoclasm and the people who carried out the destruction are called iconoclasts.

Livre This was the currency of the time and is French for pound.

Lit de justice The personal attendance by the king in *parlement* in order that an unpopular edict, in this case Amboise, be registered. On the one hand it was symbolic of the king's majority but on the other it demonstrated the unwillingness of *parlement* to ratify any legislation that offered toleration to Huguenots.

Mini ice age The mini ice age refers to a period of climatic change in sixteenth century Europe during which time annual mean temperatures across Europe fell. This resulted in significant falls in agricultural production.

Nepotism is getting jobs for one's family.

The nobility of the robe A new noble class that emerged in the sixteenth century that owed its status to wealth rather than birth. Merchants made good or landowners that had struck rich purchased royal offices and titles, thus entering the noble estate.

The nobility of the sword The established nobility in France who were closely related to the crown and inherited their noble title. Many were extremely powerful. The nobility of the sword did service to the king on the battlefield and raised armies in his name. In return, they were exempted from all taxation.

Ordinance of Montpellier Law which required all printers and booksellers to deliver a copy of every new book to the royal librarian at Blois.

Parlements The *parlements* were sovereign law courts that acted as royal courts of appeal. *Parlements* therefore heard legal grievances involving the king and were expected to uphold the king's will. Royal legislation or edicts were also endorsed and ratified by *parlements* before becoming law.

Pluralism is holding a number of clerical posts at once.

Politiques Describes those in favour of religious coexistence in order to ensure stability. The term was only really used after 1584.

Provincial estates Representative assemblies held in some areas throughout France that guarded the particular rights and privileges of those areas.

Provincial liberties Many cities, towns and provinces had been granted special conditions by the crown that allowed them to be exempt from taxation or to erect internal trade barriers.

Remonstrance A formal protest issued by *parlement* against an edict that it disagrees with and refuses to ratify.

Renaissance monarchy Renaissance monarchs are those in the fifteenth and sixteenth centuries who embraced the rebirth of classical literature and artistic styles that occurred throughout Europe. In France the period 1498–1559 is viewed as the high point of Renaissance monarchy.

Royal household Attended to the needs of the king, through three main departments. The chapel met the king's spiritual needs; the chamber ran the day-to-day affairs of the king's bedchamber; the hotel fed the court.

Salic law The fundamental laws of the French monarchy dictating succession. Heretics and women were excluded from the succession by Salic law.

The Sixteen The urban based Catholic League in Paris.

The Sorbonne The Sorbonne was a college of the University of Paris, in particular the theological faculty.

The *taille* The main direct tax in France levied on those who could afford to pay least, namely the third estate (or peasantry).

Tax farming Local taxes were collected by individuals who had paid for a contract from the crown to do so. The crown was assured of revenues; the tax farmers could make enormous profits for themselves.

The third estate All those who did not belong to the clergy and the nobility. At the top end of the third estate were wealthy merchants and landowners. The majority of the third estate were peasants living off the land.

Triumvirate A military alliance of three key noblemen.

Vulgate Bible The Latin translation of the Christian Bible which became the official Latin text of the Catholic Church.

INDEX